THE ECONOMICS QUINCUNX

I0396498

DAVID GREEN, B. Sc. (Econ)

published by JOHN NYE TEAMWORK

john.nye1@talktalk.net

ISBN #:	978-1-291-38794-0
Content ID:	13791983
Book Title:	The Economics Quincunx

DEDICATION

In memory of the London School of Economics as it was under Carr-Saunders and of my professor there, Lionel Robbins, who, God bless him, taught us that there is no such thing as either left-wing nor right-wing economics, and that economics won't tell us what to do, but merely tell us that if we want this, we should try doing that....

It was said, probably correctly, that the School was something of a disappointment to Sidney and Beatrice Webb, its founders, but in point of fact if we were to want the sort of society the Webbs advocated, economics will only tell us how to get there. I do believe Bernard Shaw, their close friend, understood that. He was certainly "big" enough to see that people like Jevons had scored a point over Marx. May I also recall the non-academic library endowed by Charlotte Payne-Townsend, Shaw's wife, where I spent much of my time.

D.G.

CONTENTS

SHORT BIBLIOGRAPHY

The Nature and Significance of Economic Science, Lionel Robbins

Prelude in Economics, Christopher Budd

Survey of Contemporary Economics, The American Economic Association , 1950

Kerapunkte des sozialen Fragen, Rudolf Steiner (neither of the two English translations of this book is reliable)

The Scottish Enlightenment, Arthur Herman

Cambridge Biographical Encyclopaedia,

ed David Crystal, entry for Heraclitus, (Heracleitos)

The Man who gave his Company away, Susanna Hoe

Robinson Crusoe, Daniel Defoe,

The Nature of Capitalist Crisis, John Strachey.

Major Barbara, George Bernard Shaw.

An easy way to find most of these books is to go to a bookfinder, who will go through the lists of books put out by second-hand bookshops on the internet for you. Bookfinders can be found in yellow pages. I go myself to Glyns Books in Ellesmere

WARNING TO READERS

You will not get far by leafing through what follows and digesting mere snippets of "information".

Information is useless without analysis; because we live in an uncertain and continually changing world

And all analysis is controversial because it requires taking a position, making propositions which are to be continually checked against future events.

What this book offers you then, is questions as much as answers. Different analysts will give different answers to specific questions. The use of analysis is that, at least, it focuses attention on what may be the key questions. Moreover in economics the possible answers are always conditional, often relate to things, which are hard to measure, and even to factors, which are intrinsically unquantifiable.

PREFACE

At sometime in the past the Senate of the University of London seemingly decided that economics must be a science.

They were mistaken.

Economics is mere theory. It cannot be anything else. To be more precise, it is philosophy. Just that. You cannot really "apply" philosophy; "applying" your chosen philosophy takes you out of the realm of philosophy altogether and into the realm of decision making.

Those economists who in the past have set up, for example, the apparatus of government economic statistics, had perforce to decide to ignore the divergence which can develop between the "real" economy and its money reflection: eg they have to decide what is an "industry" so that existing firms can be grouped into "industries", often enough they find that real companies straddle the imaginary boundary line between one "industry" and another. Statistics appear to be about economics, but this is really a semantic illusion.

"Applied" economics tends to leave the true field of economics. I have to question whether it is really wise to teach a subject called "applied economics".

By doing so, we produce people who can call themselves economists but have an imperfect grasp of the analytical theory they seek to "apply". The relationship between "pure" and "applied" cannot be the same as it is in a proper science like, say, physics.

Being an economist axiomatically implies having a "role relationship" with non-economists. All my degree means is that I have been through a sort of symbolic initiation into that role-relationship. In my now quite long life I have always worked as a business economist. Even when I did for a while teach economics, this has only been to industrial managers. Many years ago a study by the American Brookings Institution included a remark that the role of the business economist was to "open the doors of thought to the simplest proposition in the text books". Note that **all** sound propositions in economics have necessarily to be fairly simple! Any proposition which is complex should be regarded with suspicion.

Academic economists are there to teach others to become economists. But I suspect that they run serious risks if they attempt, qua academics, to involve themselves too much in practical business, let alone in advising government on policy making. This is because, in looking at the economy, they very understandably contrast it with how, in their theory, it "should" be. A business economist dare not do that!. S/he must consider the world as it is, not as it should be! All an economist can truly be is to act as a sort of priest to the world of work, that world which a German has so sensibly called the "Wirtschaftsleben."

Ancient Greek philosophy told us that if we want to know about horses, we should go to someone who has had continual dealings with horses. One of my daughters has had such dealings, and she once told me that, in show jumping, a horse which jibs at a jump does so because it is afraid it is going to die.

She cannot of course "know" any such thing. She cannot know what a horse actually thinks or feels. But she has watched so many horses continually and has discussed them with other people who have done the same thing.

Dear reader, what I can tell you about economic life is much the same sort of thing as what my daughter has told me about horses. It comes from what I have observed, using the analysis that Lionel Robbins taught me years ago. I can at least claim a lot of practice! I went up to university not yet 18 and as I sit down to write this book I am nearly 83. As most of my fellow students had fought in the war, and were anything up to 10 years older than me, I could probably claim to have watched the economy longer than any now living economist! And yet, if I am to be honest, I have to say that only recently have I felt I had a sure enough touch to attempt such a book as this. That is the sort of subject economics is! It is very important for you to try and understand that! And I am going to put forward a positively outrageous claim, namely that business economists are the only **real** economists! Truly "academic" economists should be extremely careful what they say to the general public. A business economist, as I have already suggested has to go by the jokey maxim I have seen pinned up on a factory wall – "Ensure brain is engaged before operating mouth".

I shall strive to do that – but it may lead me to say things you don't like ....

D. G. October 2012 Calais

1. WHAT IS ECONOMICS FOR?

There is no one right analysis. Choice between different analyses is a matter of judgment, perhaps even of instinct. A good analysis is one that works in practice. Different analyses can sometimes work equally well. This diversity can be advantageous. (In the European Union, it might be worth trying out different analyses in different member states, and comparing results.) What we do know, *ex post, is* when an analysis is bad; because it fails to account for what happens. The proof of the pudding is in the eating.

Two different aspects of economic analysis are that a) one has to *select,* from the enormous mass of economic events, those indicators that one judges to be *significant.*

This selection can only be *subjective.*

One can attempt to improve the selection by teamwork. Different economists can each watch a different part of the economy. They` can note any unusual events and report them. This was how the Deutches Bundesbank worked in the 1960s (and probably still does.) Their system was explained to me by one of their economists, Dr Berger. His job was to watch hire purchase. But when all the reports of the team are put together, in the last analysis, some senior economist will be exercising his subjective judgment. And this applies even more strongly in the second aspect b) explaining *why* key events have happened.

All good economic analysts can and will differ. They will have interests, which influence their thinking. (In my case, the only things I really care about are poetry, Purcell's music and model railways. Hopefully, my interests cannot distort my vision too much - but that is for you, dear reader to judge.) This need to *select, judge,* and exercise mere *opinion* is intrinsic in the subject! Economics can't be constructed from mere "information". The fashion in recent years is in fact a somewhat aberrant by-product of Harvard "behaviourism". Economics has to consider itself with *role relationships.* (I tend to think that the Chicago school of social psychology is more "user friendly" for economic thinking.)

In economics, there cannot but be this mighty inherent problem of *uncertainty*! And in economics that is the heart of the problem. Governments, businesses and individuals all have to act for an unknown future. That means we all have to take *risks.* Guess right and we make a profit, perhaps a large one; guess wrong and make a *loss.* That is how the world is like it or not. The basic truths of economics are unchangeable. They relate to two fundamental situations;

a) the species as a whole has to work to live

b) we can produce much more if work is divided up into a large number of *specializations.*

Other matters are not necessarily so unalterable – concepts of ownership, the way in which money and finance are organized, the share out of the added value between government, employers and employees, the way in which entrepreneurs get and use ideas and so on. All these things can change all the time in almost kaleidoscopic fashion. The whole thing will remind those interested in philosophy of the propositions of Heraclitus, that the universe is a continuing series of conflicts of opposites, which are however regulated by the Logos ie by reason. Economics is somewhat of that nature. And it is reason which has to apply the two basic truths mentioned in whatever situation arises. How this application should proceed is a matter of *opinion.* It has been well said that if two economists discuss something they will reflect at least 4 opinions. That is as it should be. Simply because of change and uncertainty, governments have to determine economic policies, but widely differing economic policies sometimes seem to have much the same effect in different countries. Presumably, different policies have not affected the key determinants of events as much as governments had expected: the economy has gone its own way in spite of any policy!

Government polices tend to reflect the interests of the groups that have put them in power. But events tend to be finally determined by the interaction of all interests in the economy, not just some. Throughout history, various different economic systems have been set up. But the purpose of all economic systems is to enable the survival of the species. Are the apparent differences in these various systems as important as we like to think? Maybe what we see as "system" is only a superficial aspect.

Systems can fail. For example it has been suggested that the Maya civilization depended on the cultivation of the spirulina algae (still eaten in parts of Africa); and that some crop failure led to its collapse. In recent times, there was the failure of the potato crop in nineteenth century Ireland.

Governments can be driven to very drastic actions by threats to the food supply. Stalin's policy of collectivization of agriculture was motivated by the fear of famine, as was the Japanese invasion of China, when the post -1929 tariff wars made iit hard to provide food by foreign trade. It is now common for the international community to act purposefully when there are local famines in Africa. So it is not unreasonable to say that the minimalization of government interference in the economy does involve, among other things, a successful food policy. The economic system must keep the population fed, and moreover clothed and housed. How is it that the economic system can normally do this without government help? And yet there is sometimes great and unpredictable uncertainty in this "basic" part of the economy.

We are **addicted** to wrong analyses. Because they hide from us the truths we'd rather not confront.

Only a rigorous chain of reasoning will expose a wrong analysis *ex ante.* But *ex post* we will find out the hard way – if it is wrong; it won't work! Mere snippets of information, no matter in what quantity, do not of themselves join together to form a chain of reasoning. We have to think things through. We really should get back to a culture of rigorous economic reasoning. This may even require *ignoring* the snippets! But it might stop us from making costly mistakes.

A 20th century position in philosophy, about the use of history, has affected economics, that of Popper. He attacked what he called "historicism". He argued that you don't have to know a things history to understand it.

But for this to be true, you must be sure you are able to understand it **without** knowing its history! In practice, this is often rather difficult, because reality can be so very complex. It can be beyond the human minds ability to grasp it fully. I myself believe that most minds have difficulty in thinking about more than five inter-related things at once – so to think about a really complex reality requires simplification (what is called "abstraction"). One has to judge which are the key things and analyze these. This is why analysis is so important. We cannot in practice use "information" except by fitting it into an analysis. Too much information actually swamps our minds – so too much information can even be worse than useless! We have to lose our fear of making generalizations: because in practice we cannot do without them. If economists ignore this they run a grave risk of becoming I like Swift's Laputians in "Gulliver's Travels" – a race of intellectual professors who were so addicted to "pure thought" that they had to have minders to stop them walking into obstacles. To highlight this risk some professors of economics have made the maximum simplification possible, by using Robinson Crusoe as an example of economic life. There is some truth in this: Daniel Defoe can be seen as the first economist before Adam Smith! But we shouldn't overdo it. Some economic prepositions necessitate there being more than one person involved.

You won't find the answer to the economic problems of our time on the internet. Don't ask me why: I dont know. But it must be so, because if the answers were there, wouldn't somebody have found them, told governments, and the problems would have been solved. My own hypothesis is that we have forgotten things we once knew.

Hence this book.

This kind of collective *oubli* can happen. I was sent one of those rather dull magazines put out by Jehovah's Witnesses. This one was better than usual. It contained a glowing account of how science, medicine, philosophy and history flourished under Haroun al Rashid I was able to link this with one of the essays written by the French free-thinker Renan (to be found in his book "Celtic Poetry"). He showed how Bagdad had declined: he said this was due to growing fundamentalism of the Muslim rulers of what is now Iraq. This is possibly unfair: yet he has been there, and cited discussions he had had with Moslems living there. The whole brilliant culture faded. Was that why Bagdad succumbed to the Turkish invaders? I can't tell you, but maybe we should look at that bit of history, to see if we can find any clues to our present malaise.

But we've probably got to do more ferreting than that. Perhaps we should ransack our own western past? There are ten million or so books published in English since printing started. Perhaps we should see them as a sort of lucky dip? "Search engines" now are very systematized, but what they produce is snippets. No answers there, as I say But what would we be looking for? My whole training and experience tells me that what we need is a simple chain or network of related ideas. That is what provides one with analysis.

In economics, a limited question may only need a couple of ideas to answer it. Let me give you an example from my work at Ford, Dagenham. Every year we got the annual report and accounts of various car manufacturers. The Volkswagen accounts came to me. What was wanted was a one page note of their profit for the year 1960. It had to be an estimate because the account did not show profit. I believe this was normal in Germany at the time. I made an estimate using only two or three known facts. They had a similar production technology to Ford. The Beetle car was similar in size to the Anglia, then in production. They made only the Beetle. (We had several different models). Using the idea of economies of scale, I worked out what our profit would have been if we had only made Anglias, and had made as many as the Germans had made Beetles. This gave me an estimate of the profit. If I recall rightly, I made it about £1 million. I took my note into my director, John Barber. He looked me in the eye and said "Are you sure of this?" I said "Yes". And he signed the report and it went to the English Ford directors and the American company. He had far more experience than I did and he judged it to be OK.

Current economic questions are far more weighty, of course. But economics offers the same sort of broad-brush treatment of them. We are looking for a set of inter-related ideas. At the LSE in 1947 -50 I was given such a set.

I believe that any decent economist working today could make an extremely useful analysis using these ideas, and could advise governments what to do. I have read a recent speech by Mervyn King, governor of the Bank of England; this speech showed he was not getting such advice.

This book reiterates what I was taught. Let me give an example of how it might be used, one current question to be resolved is about world trade; how is an *optimum* distribution of *economic* activity to be achieved across the whole planet?

A theoretical analysis can be produced to suggest that if there is worldwide free trade, an optimum distribution will, *over a period,* result. In an optimum distribution each district or region would produce the things it is best fitted to produce, and these would be exchanged with the things it was not so good at producing. With natural resources, this can seem fairly reasonable. Some countries have oil, others copper, others tropical fruit and so on. But when it comes to *industrial* products, modern industrial production technologies are quite footloose. The same types of factory can be built pretty well anywhere, with the same built-in labour productivities. That being the case, there ought not to be any cost advantage in one country as against another. And the cost to that country of keeping a labour supply available ought to be fairly similar everywhere, because human needs for nutrition, shelter, clothing, heating and health services should also be much the same throughout the planet.

So when there are *apparent* differences in such costs, one has to suspect a *hidden cause. This can only be in the monetary system.* Such apparent differences are very likely to result from currency exchange rate *anomalies,* such as one currency being over- or under- valued against another.

Such currency anomalies may take a very long time to smooth out through competition, unless such competition can effectively iron out anomalous price differences in for example rents or foods. But that may often be almost impossible, because there are many obstructions to the free sale or purchase of land, and to the import or export of basic food stuffs. The problem is that the money system is rather far from reflecting the *purchasing power* of each currency, for ordinary people living in the area it covers. This is because prices reflect the volumes of supply and demand *within* each region. Large countries still tend to be largely *self-contained,* and world trade is not particularly likely to change this fact, except in the very long run.

I was able to observe something of this sort when serving in the Army in Egypt. The camp I worked at employed Egyptian workers. The were paid 5 piastres a day. One hundred piastres made an Egyptian pound (very slightly more than an English pound at that time). As a sergeant I was paid about £8 per week and had of course my food and clothing all found. On five hundredths of a pound how did they stay alive? Well, they did. They came back to work the next morning! The answer lay in the fact that food prices were *correspondingly* low; so low in fact that the Egyptian coinage had to be divided into thousandths of a pound! (so that these prices could be paid)

Another important concept in economics – but one which requires imagination to apply – is that of **optimum** size. One ought to be able to make shrewd guesses at the optimum sizes for:-

a) a firm in any given industry

b) a political unit (considering the costs of necessary government and the economies of scale in government functions)

c) an economy – ie an area in which there was free movement of goods, people, firms, money. Probably such an economy will need to have a single currency within its limits.

A special kind of study would need to be done to make reasonably sound estimates of optimum size, estimates one could "live with". But one might for example find, that the optimum size of a firm varied greatly between different sectors of the economy.

There is really no such thing as "applied economics". The subject works the other way round. We all observe, nay experience, economic events. From these observations we try to work out our economic theories. True, economists do often say that these theories demand that we do certain things, eg in the field of economic policies. These only work if the premises of the theories apply. Any change in circumstances, any change at all, will throw stress on the theory and may be render it inapplicable.

So, (as of now it would seem) we get combinations of events which don't fit the theories, it is the theories that have to change as we cant change the events. This is particularly true of what is called "econometrics" – the attempt to make mathematical formulae out of *quantities.* Suppose, just suppose, that some economic causes are **qualities,** not quantities at all? ...

I once heard a monk define a mystery as something you could go on thinking about for all eternity and never quite get to the bottom of. It seems to me that *quality* is such a mystery. And that therefore all things which are qualitative partake of mystery. I am conscious that not everyone will agree. Many will prefer to share the Marxist view (see Stalin's *Dialectical and Historical Materialism)* that "quality" is somehow the final result of some process which is inherently quantitative in nature.

Many economists of all persuasions, eg Marx, Jevons, Keynes have all refused to consider quality at all! (for an attempt to grapple with this at a philosophical level – see Robert Pirsig's book "Zen and the Art of Motorcycle Maintenance".) Economics being a form of philosophy has to take the problem of quality on board. Economists need to recall that many basic concepts – utility, value, entrepreneurialism, capital, etc – are inherently qualitative, and can scarcely be quantified at all. If this Is not remembered, error must result.

And over all this looms yet another knotty problem: the universe is far more complex than our mental processes. Man is the most complex object in the whole universe; and economics is to do with the role relationships between these highly complex objects we call people. Yet whenever we try to complexify our thought processes, we are prone to further significant error.

Dear reader, are you beginning to see why, in our present world, economics has come to be such a crucial subject? Much governmental and world institutional activity has to be guided by the advice of economists. So political leaders need a checklist, so that they can verify that their advisors have thought carefully about *all* the main factors.

(1) Economics is about work.

(2) A notable characteristic of human work is that the total global amount of it is divided and sub- divided, and subdivided again and again into myriad specialities, each with its own particular skills and know-how.

(3) In order to combine these specialities, we have to exchange them. And for that we need money which leads us to the snag – more than a mere snag, rather it is a fundamental philosophical difficulty. While money is perceived as *measuring* value, value is a *quality.*

Money hides from us the very simple fact that different people put a different valuation on the same thing.

(1) Producers value the money they hope to gain more than the things they make.

(2) Consumers buy things they value more than what they have to pay out.

That is how exchange works. But if we hope that money is a sort of yardstick, it is only the measuring rod for some sort of compromise between opposing valuations, which in themselves are inherently not commensurable, because they are subjectively perceived qualities. The intervention of money between these qualities gives us a totally spurious illusion of objectivity. While the government needs yardsticks for working out its economic policies, the brutal truth is that money is a very protean yardstick.

I repeat, the consumer values the pint he buys in a pub more than the cash he gives the barmaid. But what is meant by that simple word "more"? Face this awkward philosophical problem, dear reader, that "more" is inherently **unquantifiable.** My teachers at the LSE in 1947-50 did try to get round this by a curious system of notional graphs, called supply and demand curves. But both the professors and we students knew in our hearts that this was a bit cock-eyed. The last time I saw Lionel Robbins, it was some years after graduating, about a reference, I mentioned to him that I had had problems with the subject. He asked "I suppose you found it unreal". I had to reply "Yes"

The development of the world economy has created a vast range of commodities, which never existed in previous centuries. Only a "free enterprise" economy can produce the massive list of items in something like the right quantities As each region of the world gets into closer contact with the world economic culture, it experiences a Wirtschaftswunder (miracle), usually for a decade or so, though the first one in England must have lasted longer. (Only the governmental habit of amassing statistics didn't commence until after it was over, so we have little information about it.) By the time it was over Germany, Japan and America all had enormous ones. A less well-known one was the Soviet one in the1930s.

As I write, it seems to be the turn of Brazil, Russia, India and China. We can probably look forward to ones in say Turkey, or Egypt, or South Africa. (My list is not of course exhaustive.) Why these short-lived periods of rapid economic growth peter out is something of a mystery. No doubt this will be studied by economists one day. I suspect a complex of causes. New enterprises require an unmeasurable quality, namely imagination. So maybe it is a cultural factor which is at work, when the wells of creative inspiration deep in our subconscious minds seem to run dry. But an obvious cause is the development of oligopoly, when a small number of very large firms tend to grip hard on the process of competition and either eliminate rivals or take them over. Another factor in the past has been the export of capital, highlighted by Lenin, but we are now in a situation where there are fewer and fewer places so underdeveloped that it is attractive to export capital to them. Moreover, the exhaustion of scarce mineral deposits in remote places is going to have a similar effect. I suspect oligopoly is going to break up, but I could be wrong.

Economics I repeat is philosophy. It's because we dont understand that, that we continually get it all wrong. Philosophy is in my definition a guide to action in uncertainty. Economics is about action in uncertainty.

We need economics to guide people how to act in the economy. Particularly the entrepreneurs who, ever since Adam Smith, have been recognized as the mainspring of the economic system. (Yet it is fairly safe to suppose that most entrepreneurs have never read a book on economics in their lives! Why is that?) But all entrepreneurs have a philosophy as I define the term. Probably or should I say usually it is one of their own making. So bringing economics back to its proper place in human thought might even, one day if not immediately, help them ...

So can we begin to see what economics is for? Simple "economic" ideas can be found in the ancient Greek philosophy which still moulds western thought. But it was with the development of industry that governments began to take various actions which impacted on business. . Once this started, people who were essentially philosophers started to develop what we now call economics. Its historical purpose was to attempt to influence and guide government policy. From Adam Smith through to Keynes and on to the economic development theorists of the fifties and sixties, this aim has continued. I believe we are now at a stage where some further development of economics is needed, to guide not only governments but also international bodies, because new problems have arisen. This would require some new economic thinker to set to work on an attempt to think through these problems in a more systematic way.

Until that happens governments will still have to muddle through, and they should at least be aware that we do not as yet have a complete set of economic doctrines which can be relied upon, as if economics were an exact science. It isn't. This will mean that some aspects of government policy must be seen as *experimental.* Governments need to understand this, and so need to do much more to monitor the effects of their actions.

But they will also find that areas of policy are escaping examination from the standpoint of tried and tested economic theories. This too needs to be rectified. In recent years it has been forgotten that key concepts such as utility, entrepreneurship, capital even, are not quantifiable. Any theory of economics should be a guide to running a business as well as to government policy making. But until the philosophical limitations of the subject are grasped, economic advice cannot be properly used or understood.

A very important causal relationship in the economy is that between capital and employment. But this too cannot be quantified; because **real** capital is not in itself quantifiable. *Real* capital must embody an *idea.* A constant flow of new ideas is needed; but whether we get them depends on the *quality* of current thinking and on the ability of entrepreneurs to do new things. To grasp this firmly we need to focus on the newness of new projects. The world is continually changing; newness is the crest of the wave of change. The best entrepreneurs are those who can detect something new in the situation and have the nous to exploit it. But the results of what they do cannot but vary all the time.

So where is this rather discursive chapter getting to? Maybe economics is useful for forecasting? A couple of years ago an academic economist, I forget his name, at Trinity College, Dublin was to be found confessing in the *Irish Times* that he hadn't foreseen a change in the housing market.

Obviously both he and some people, who had criticized him, thought he ought to have done.

Not all that long after, the so-called "Financial Crisis" broke. It wasn't foreseen. It is fairly clear to me that any economists involved in preparing the Lisbon Treaty did not foresee it. No less a person than the Queen of England asked why the crisis was not foreseen. Has anyone really answered her?

If we have a good understanding of the economic system, shouldn't we be able to foresee crises? When the National Institute of Economic and Social Research was founded, it put on the back cover of its journal, a warning that the workings of the economy were "imperfectly understood". That was in the 1960s. Would any of the present generation of economists disagree?

Economics has in fact been impacted for some150 years by some philosophically unsound analysis. This happened because the wealthy - who finance academia, one way or another, either directly or else through taxation – came to think it threatened them, and would continue to do so unless its natural line of development was deviated! This is why to day – as Greens never tire of pointing out – orthodox academic economics isn't all that good at costing damage to the environment. However, Greens tend to throw the baby out with the bath water; they have not given any real attention to the problem of detecting and rectifying the analytical flaws.

The same situation applies to the Christian critique of economic theory; there is some sharp criticism of our present society from at least some Christian quarters, attacking it as based on greed. This criticism might lead us to a clue, where to look for the flaw, did we but remember that Adam Smith the founder of economics, did so as an analyst of *morals.* To him, economics and morals are inextricably linked, virtually the same subject; linked that is by the sort of unity of opposites, which the ancient Greek philosopher Heracleitos seems to have been pointing to. Has economics become a sort of morality of greed? We are as good as told in so many words, that it is our *duty* or at least the duty of businessmen, to be as greedy as possible because that way lies "efficiency".

Now the concept of efficiency is borrowed from physics. It is based on *measurement*; efficiency relates measured quantities to each other. But what is it in economics that we are measuring? We have divided the subject into two branches only because in each branch the answer has seemed to be quite different. Thus we have;

a) "microeconomics", which deals with the formation of any piece for any one commodity taken in isolation

b) "macroeconomics" which deals with the necessities of various key limitations on the total of *all* economic activities. Usually this total is seen as being for any given national state; this produces further anomalies because the best "logical" procedure would be to work on the total for the whole planet. But it is necessary in practice because the chief use of macroeconomics is to guide each national government on policy making.

The attentive reader will have noticed I put the word "logical" in inverted commas. I did this to draw attention to a further analytical problem. In life, we have continuous movement – as Heracleitos seems to have noticed. But formal logic can only deal with things which **don't** move: we have neglected to develop a logic of movement, of change. (Perhaps Heracleitos did? We dont know, as all but a few scattered fragments of his ideas have been lost to us)

Maybe economics needs such a logic. To meet this need, there is a formal body of mathematical models, using algebraic equations. The problem with these is the very basic question already posed – what exactly are we measuring? Unless we can answer that, do we need a logic of movement which does not require measurement? That may be difficult to answer, because we may need to base our analysis on variables having a clear, conceptual existence but which are not easily measureable, perhaps even intrinsically, certainly in any useable practice.

One thing about change: someone has to manage it. So someone has to somehow foresee it, and moreover foresee it just before it has really got under way at all. We have christened the rather specialized and often distinctly odd people who do this, entrepreneurs. Whether or not our analytical system measures change, entrepreneurship has to do it for the whole planet. There isn't anyone else – well, is there? Measurement we understand. Change we daily see. But what exactly is an entrepreneur? Can we all be entrepreneurs or only some of us? If the latter, how do we relate entrepreneurs to non-entrepreneurs? Is an entrepreneur necessarily one individual or can there be such a thing as an entrepreneurial group? How can governments influence entrepreneurs? To what extent should they try to influence them: or should they leave them alone? Can we do without them altogether?

These prove to be quite tricky questions made more intractable by the fact that they seem to be all inter-related. It is indeed entrepreneurship that makes economics such a difficult subject. Yet there is one more difficulty I have not yet come to mention. It is generally agreed that an entrepreneur must have access to what we call capital. But what exactly *is* capital? Can it be measured, and if so how? Can it be measured in the same units as other economic quantities?

Lastly there is the question of *motivation* . How do we involve ourselves in economic activity? Do we do it in the right way, or could our way of involvement be improved? Can governments play any part in any improvement? And what really is "improvement"? How do we define it? Can we measure it, and if so how? Our system of income distribution relates to these questions because it has been thought that all involvement in economic activity is not one way related to income, to possible or actual changes in income, and so to incentives. Here too we may need to question the *idée's recue* of commonly fashionable concepts.

In short, economics is as complex as life itself. Doesn't this necessitate that economics be a branch of philosophy? Or is it a separate subject within itself, not related to other disciplines? Over the centuries, different economists have given varying answers to all these questions. The history of thought is in itself as complex as the rest of all this is.

I hope I have said enough for the moment to show that we *do need* economics to show us *why* these problems occur; but that it is our own *political* action which must attempt to put right anything which we find to be wrong. And of course our own business actions; if we set up sustainable activities, and find out how to make them compete effectively, we could at least start to win the battle.

2. WORK

Sometimes, notably in the late 19th century economists, workers and consumers are contrasted almost as if they were different groups of people. That of course is nonsense. We work in order to consume; we need to consume in order to be able to work. To be a worker is to enter into one role relationship: to be a consumer is to enter into another. A notable characteristic of the human species is the number of roles any one person can play. Most people work and all people consume. Obvious, isn't it? Yet one still hears people talking as if it was not obvious.

The total of economic events, what is called on the continent the "conjuncture", is made up by the total of all individual actions. An important thing to realize about the economy is that every action has *multiple* economic effects. We tend to be only aware of *one* of them, namely the effect we seek; and so we tend not to notice the other effects, but they are there! Thus it is that a total of actions can appear like "anonymous market forces". *We are all market forces.* If only people with enough money form the *apparent* forces on the stock markets, every company's fortunes are determined by the total of human actions affecting it – the actions of its workers, of its suppliers, of its customers, of its government, of its bankers, and of course of its shareholders. And its management further affects matters by the quality of its responses. In its first phase, a company has an entrepreneur, who can shape its future out of his actions; but in later phases, it has passed in to the hands of managers.

It becomes rather less productive, since they tend simply to run what they have inherited. This may be why the job of the economist seems to be to tell people things they do not want to hear – precisely because the economist is trained to observe *all* the effects of any action – including any *counter-productive* ones. This is as true of work as of any other factor in the quincunx. In economics, as no doubt in other subjects, few if any generalizations have universal application (including this one). Work is extremely variable and not so easy to define. The myth in the beginning of Genesis tells us that man must eat his bread in the sweat of his brow. But some people don't, eg the rich, those on social security, remote tropical islanders where the fruits of nature are enough to live on, and so on. But for the species as a whole the myth is true. *Enough* people must sweat to produce bread for *all.* That has always been true ever since the advent of the human species on the planet. (Economics, being about human work, has no need to concern itself with the intriguing philosophical question, whether what other species do is "work" or not.)

If some humans don't work, their relationships with those who do is just another role relationship. It enters into the field of economics because the total "added value" produced in any given economy has to be divided up. And although the myth of Genesis only seems to refer to manual work, there were already other kinds of work in existence at the time this biblical text is supposed to have been written: there were rulers, soldiers, judges, and of course the very first white collar workers, the scribes. The division of the added value between those who do different kinds of work and those who do not work at all, has always been an *issue* in all known human societies. Different societies have handled it in somewhat different ways.

But some characteristics of work cannot change whatever the society. Work has to be measured in *time.* If more can be produced in a given time by effecting changes of method, that is an improvement in "productivity". *We only have so much time, which limits our work, unless productivity can be improved.* The methods of improving productivity (output per hour per worker) vary significantly. They can be classified under three heads:-

a) Division of labour. Individual members of the workforce specialize in quite small tasks in the sequence of production leading to assembly line production in many cases.

b) Increasing the scale of operations, for example by increasing factory size. In some industries there are very important economies to be achieved in this way, called "economies of scale".

c) Developing machinery which can use less labour, by what is called automation. This requires massive expenditure. Initially high, this expenditure is often somewhat reduced in second-generation machines, as they can usually be perfected after some working experience.

The division of labour is quite old. Around the beginning of the Christian era, the large-scale manufacture of pagan artifacts centered around Ephesus, in ancient Greece. I wonder if Heracleitos noticed it? Ephesus was his hometown, and the logos, reason, has to be employed in working out the division of labour; and we do know that Heracleitos thought that the logos somehow "regulated" change. Many centuries later, the Scottish professor of moral philosophy, Adam Smith, analyzed the division of labour in some detail.

And of course in the 20th century Henry Ford used it in his assembly line production, thereby creating an enormous enterprise, an outstanding example of the economies of scale.

British Ford would have expanded as much as Volkswagen had the original Common Market included Britain from the outset. Instead Britain's being outside was the main cause of Henry Ford diverting capital projects from Ford Dagenham to Ford Koln – because he could thereby realize greater economies of scale. Incidentally the then British Motor Corporation could then have done far more to achieve economies of scale had it been better managed. Amalgamating former competitors by a merger didn't work. They went on fighting each other to their mutual detriment.

To get the full benefit from economies of scale requires ruthless and efficient top management and sophisticated financial controls. Such controls were introduced into the American Ford company by the so called Harvard "whizz-kids" among whom was MacNamara , later Kennedy's Secretary of

State. To utilize such economic concepts effectively needs vision and enterprise.

Of course to utilize it fully does require a *large* economy. Ireland is an example of a small country which has had a period of good economic growth; but it could have done even better had it had a bigger population. The island is capable of supporting a reasonably industrialized population 4 times its present size, with consequent larger market size and larger opportunities for the division of labour and so for economies of scale.

The development of automation in the motor industry has been particularly remarkable in the closing decades of the old millennium. The assembly lines now work very significantly with robotic machinery. Readers might like to note that the word "robot" derives from the Czech word for "work". Some visionaries have predicted that work as we know it would be abolished by robots – but as robots need considerable human servicing, and have to be manufactured, it is more likely such automation will only achieve a less than proportionate reduction in the total industrial work force, a reduction likely to be further offset by increases in the headcount employed in services. With all these technological advances, the fundamental truths about work remain the same.

In spite of all the ways in which productivity can be raised, there are limits. Any one nation sees only a part of the world total, being only one piece in the planet's economic jigsaw puzzle. All those pieces have to be put together to make the overall picture, *which we need to see!* There is an absolute limit on economic activity provided by the size of the planet. We are not really near that limit yet, but one day we might be. No more minerals are to be mined than there are in the earth to be got. No harvest can be gathered except from the fertile areas. And some fertile land is already used for other purposes. London has been built on some of the most fertile land in the country. And even in remoter areas there are, for example, motorways. These take up more space than the old-fashioned railways. Might we one day have to go back to the railway and plough up the motorways? Well, maybe not yet! But one absolute limit imposes itself each day: no more hours can be worked than there are people to work them. That is why it is so silly to tolerate unemployment, *which limits the common wealth of those in work.* If the unemployed could get jobs, more could be produced, and we could all share in that more. Why doesn't the economic system do something about that?

A good question. We try to understand it. We argue about it. Sometimes we come to blows over our arguments. Various social institutions have been set up throughout history to cope with it. People who have a better understanding of what is happening have an advantage over those who do not. The possibility is always there of turning this better understanding to their own advantage, and this can - and very often does – generate conflict. But none of us have as good an understanding of it all as we could wish. We all have to grasp these limits:

- the total amount of things on the planet available to our use

- the total amount of hours which can be worked in any given period

- therefore the total *real* income which can be created in any year.

There are other things which are difficult to alter for social rather than material reasons. These things relate to how the total income is shared out between us all. This sharing out is very complex, but the first thing to realize is that it *could* be done in many different ways – if there were general social agreement on how to change the existing system. Politics is about trying to obtain sufficient agreement to make such changes, though most politicians are content to let things go on as they are, because that is how they get elected – and maybe that is OK? As it is, by strongly entrenched social conventions, the sharing out process is done, in each productive unit, by a system of contracts, very often given in "corporate" form. These contracts allocate income to different groups in various ways. But the total amount of income to be shared out is at least in the short term, pretty well *fixed; so* that if our method of allocation pays out more than there really is in the kitty, there will be problems.

All social conventions depend on the predominant philosophy in society. A large part of what economics studies is to do with such social conventions. Might a different philosophy to what is currently in vogue not tend to develop different social conventions? Or are these conventions rooted in timeless universal truths? Man is a political animal, as Aristotle observed. There is a boundary between politics and economics. In answering the above questions, there has to be movement in both direction, but we need to keep in mind where the frontier is. Nowhere is this more true than in the matter of work. (The small change of politics is often about striking more or less tendentious philosophical attitudes. Which is however not to say that a philosophically viable politics is impossible!)

Various groups in economic life employ an economist in the same way as they would employ a lawyer – as an *advocate.* If you do not realize this you will find economics a very confusing subject; once you realize it, it becomes quite easy to master.

Before passing on to the next chapter, I ought to perhaps mention "work study". This was very fashionable in industry in the first three quarters of the 20th century. But a widely-used invention of the last quarter shows little sign of having been work-studied! The p c keyboard lacks good ergonomic design. It is not clear why this has not yet been rectified.

3. CAPITAL

The real capital of any business is the sum total of the abilities of all the people in it. These abilities can often only be exercised with the aid of capital equipment and extensive "premises" space. These abilities can moreover only be exercised when there is group agreement that they be exercised and in what way. While costs are directly incurred by the business in using equipment and space, these are only part of the real capital cost. *Many abilities have no direct or apparent cost.* The real capital of the business grows when the *quality of* equipment, space and agreements improves. But this cannot be quantified. Capital is really just ideas. No piece of capital equipment is worth anything except for the ideas in it – and such equipment becomes worthless when the ideas have become obsolete.

Only individuals can have ideas. So only individuals should really own capital. An individually developed capital idea is like a "copyright" – a specific formulation. It may need, probably will need, some sort of finance to become a working entity. But finance should not involve the transfer of "ownership" of the idea. *How can anyone own an idea?* Think about that. "Copyright" should really expire when the owner of the "copyright" dies. It really should not be "saleable". The idea *qua* idea should pass back to the community at large, because ideas are essentially common to the whole community. So "patenting" is fundamentally wrong, and should be abolished. There should only be inalienable copyright expiring with the real "owners" death. It becomes rather less productive, since they tend simply to run what they have inherited. This may be why the job of the economist seems to be to tell people things they do not want to hear – precisely because the economist is trained to observe *all* the effects of any action – including any *counter-productive* ones. This is as true of work as of any other factor in the quincunx. In economics, as no doubt in other subjects, few, if any, generalizations have completely universal application (including this one).

The capital ideas of any such "copyright" could then be copied by anyone on the "owners" death. It seems to me that that is fair.

Companies can of course own the physical assets embodying the copyrighted ideas, which assets will continue to have value until they become obsolete. But shares in companies should only be owned by *real* persons and not by other companies. Mergers can then only be effected when the same real persons own sufficient shares in both companies to vote the merger! Companies could be *divided* when shares passed on by inheritance or sale to real individuals who wished to divide the ownership.

I am asserting this because it seems blindingly obvious to me to do things in the existing way limits the human use of the real capital we already have. Such limitations cause – and cannot but cause – economic stagnation which harms us all, including the "patent" owners. (I put "patent" and "copyright" in inverted commas because I am not using these words in the usual way.) Incidentally, it doesn't necessarily matter all that much who owns industry. What matters is that whoever owns it manages it efficiently. Owners who do not manage their businesses efficiently will go out of business unless they correct their ways. (A nationalized industry may be better managed than a private one: in 1960 Volkswagen made a huge profit, a larger profit than any other motor manufacturer in Europe has ever made. And at that time it was nationalized! The Soviet Union had a wirtschaftswunder {miracle} in the 30s because the state-owned industry was leased out to entrepreneurs.)

An owner-entrepreneur is more likely to have a free hand in pursuing the development of *new capital ideas.* Owner-entrepreneurs are certainly best at handling *change.* Companies which pioneer change are often new companies; it is often very hard for a large established company to change sufficiently thoroughly and quickly. Of course, all companies go through a life cycle, in three phases

a) Growth when a new company is led by an entrepreneur.

b) Stable continuation with less growth or perhaps none, run more by ordinary managers.

c) Decline.

Companies in phase a) will grow if they have good capital ideas. This is why it is so important to always have many new companies starting. Economic growth must come mainly from new companies. If anything – such as excessive fuss-pot regulation – hinders the growth of new companies, we won't have much growth at all!

This initial growth should continue until the company concerned has reached its optimum size, which depends on the economies of scale. But beyond that point, it would be better if they ceased to grow, or at least growth slackened to what can be achieved by improving productivity. There is absolutely no advantage to the economy in having companies which are larger than the economies of scale really warrant. (This is why mergers and take-overs are frequently harmful.) In general terms it can be assumed that reasonably good competition between a sufficient number of companies will automatically restrict growth to something like optimum size – but if competition is imperfect, watch out! Companies in stage b) are still useful, and should stay in business for a long time if well managed. It has to be accepted that in the end, most companies will, and should die.

One obvious flaw in Marx's analysis is that while he saw very clearly how the money was found to finance capital, he did not give much attention to the fact that the money is wasted if it goes on projects of little or no use. Goods for consumption move out of the economic system before their usefulness is tested. Goods for capital use do not! Their utility - or otherwise – profoundly affects the working of the economic system. (All economic systems founder on this fact; the *effects* of any capital are unmeasurable – because, to put it simply, capital is not a quantity but a *quality*) This applies for example, to the badly designed p.c. keyboard.

In the mid-seventies, Milton Freidman did a television programme, broadcast in many countries, arguing that if we would only adopt the "free market" solutions of classical economics, all would be well. Many countries have adopted this advice, but after many decades, the results, as everyone knows, are far from good. Why is this? What went wrong?

The answer is that this classical economics contains in its thinking the *same* error as the Marxist thinking which also failed. Folkert Wilken, a farsighted man, foresaw all this before Milton Friedman had even prepared his video. His masterly book, which is however a little "difficult", is called *Capital.* I luckily got the task of translating this book, which I still publish.

In this book, he argues that the wrong handling of capital is producing all the economic calamities. Writing as an old man in a hurry to tell the world something, he warned that if we did not get this right, the world could descend into chaos. At the time this seemed a bit over the top! Can we say it is right now? The crux of his argument is that to have freedom, we must still think through more carefully what we are doing in respect of capital. Maybe he has a point?

If capital is ideas, these ideas need to be shared by the working group of a company, and moreover be reasonably well understood by the customers and government, in short by what in the anthropological sense of the word is called a culture. (It is precisely because other groups need to understand the ideas that "patenting" or "copyrighting" is so wrong headed.)

So there needs to be a measure of social cohesion. Social cohesion is based on quite "small" things, and is important economically because it impinges on capital, indeed might be seen as part of capital. Such small things may be based on "networks", on "extended families", on local geography, on whom young people tend to marry, on which pub one goes to, even, and certainly on ones religious ideas (including those religious ideas adopted by non-religious people!) I could go on.

Big things, like immigration, do tend to cause fragmentation of socially cohesive cultures. Sixty or more years ago, this fragmentation hadn't occurred. Now it has. What do we need to do about it, as far as capital is concerned?

Different "cultures" have different focal points; if, to form a company's capital, people have to work together, they do not need to change their "culture" but they do need to get a good understanding of other co-workers "cultural" ideas; because different value systems are involved. *Language incorporates value–systems, and always has done.* The Roman word "verbum" contains different value associations to the Greek word "logos". Probably the Roman Empire broke into two parts because Greeks and Romans found it difficult to work together.

Any one person is a member of the species, Homo sapiens which has been in existence over perhaps a million or more years. In that time the species has acquired habits. One habit, developed over so many generations of tribal wars, is one of initial distrust of those perceived as coming from "other" tribes. Tribes may have grown into nations, but the habit of distrust is so deeply ingrained as to persist. Perhaps it always will. But all economic relationships are based on *trust*! Knee-jerk reactions of distrust frustrate economic exchange, distort competition and hinder cooperation – and we do need all three.

You see, what I am saying is that what used to be called "labour relations" and now is termed something like "human resource management" is really an aspect of *capital* ! That's how it is. Maybe it's a pity we dont all understand that better. But you see, if capital is essentially ideas, these ideas have to be commonly understood. (This is why I find the "Chicago" school of social psychology so helpful as an economist: their notion that the human mind cannot store any idea without giving it an emotional valuation is (or so I find myself) invaluable in understanding the complex role relationships of economic life. And understanding, if the Chicago school is right, involves *emotional* activity of some kind.

If then co-workers must understand each others values for the company's real capital to function, what are we to do? One interesting answer was one I encountered in the 60s at Walls Sausage factory in Willesden. They had a very mixed labour force, ethically. So they divided it up into teams of (if I remember rightly) about nine people. In each team there was only one member of any one ethnic group! Another factory I visited in Birmingham, about the same time, had solved the problem, or should I say sought to solve it, by only having one ethnic group in any one department. I cite these examples merely to stress an overlooked "quality" of capital.

If capital is ideas, one has to be clear what exactly is an *idea.*_It is more than *information*. An idea is more about *analysis* than about information, and the analysis must be shared so it needs cohesion. In recent years we have developed a surfeit of information, but we have a corresponding *dearth* of analysis and perhaps of cohesion too. Is that why we also have a current shortage of *new* capital ideas?

As I say, it is normal as markets and technologies change that some firms close down. But it should also be normal that other new firms start up! But a new firm needs its own capital idea. Without one, no new firm can start – and to start it also needs *cohesion.*

This could be why the single market and the (mostly) single currency in the European Union has so far failed to produce many truly "European" companies, ie ones in which co-workers come from a variety of nations. Even companies in which two nations collaborate closely are rare. There have been examples in the aerospace industry: and the Arte television company significantly based in Strasbourg does provide another, but there aren't many others.

This is worrying when the "European" culture seems to have become a bit too anti-business. Many businesspersons are finding the huge mountain of European "directives" irksome. The Irish minister involved in "selling" the Lisbon treaty to the Irish electorate a second time did admit this irksomeness existed, but brushed it aside as unimportant!

But could he have been wrong? There must be some cause why so few capital ideas are emerging in Europe - because they are significantly lacking. If they weren't, we wouldn't only have slumps – we would at least some of the time also have booms! Maybe the capital idea is a *delicate* plant: are we perhaps killing it?

It has been suggested that we are creating another "command" economy like that in the former USSR. (The jibe that we now have the EUSSR has been heard!) Even the Soviet command economy could not kill all new capital ideas. I once saw a picture of a toy railway train in Soviet Russia. For such a thing to be made at all, someone had some sort of capital idea. I suspect the real reason for the collapse of the Soviet economy was not so much the command economy as the lack of competitive market. So I doubt if the Brussels command system can do quite as much harm – it *is* tempered by competition. But it does not help. Brussels directives all tend to assume that there is only one right way of doing things. But axiomatically, *any new capital idea asserts that the existing way of doing things is wrong,* and so must be changed. Such assertion may be wrong – or it may be right. *No* bureaucrat can tell in advance, ex ante! We can only find out *ex post*, by trying it out. That is what *laissez-faire* allows. Sorry Brussels – but don't we need to get back to laissez-faire? That is if we want to cultivate new capital ideas. And so build a new Europe?

Much more could be said about capital. The reader should explore the subject further, not only by reading but also by his/her own observations and thoughts. S/he may perhaps find some of the Appendix useful.

Each company is in its own unique position moving into a changing and uncertain future. In this movement, each company is always out of balance in respect of capital. There is a perpetual need to cultivate the company's capital, to make it grow, like a living thing, to meet this or that change in the situation it faces. Sometimes, some inspiration can bring about a rapid growth in capital in a very short time.

At other times, long years of cultivation may yield only a meagre result. (I should point out that "growth" for capital is rather like growth for a plant; it is a living thing, as I say, so that growth is not so much quantitative as qualitative.)

Here endeth the lesson!

4. VALUE

There has never been such unanimity amongst economists as there was in the immediate aftermath of the publication of Marx's *Capital.* Just for once, all economists' insight said the same thing. Forgive me being nostalgic, but the best lecture I ever heard in my student days was a brilliant one by Lionel Robbins. He made great fun with the way in which economic gurus of different nationalities each displayed national characteristics in the way they said things – *but each said the same point*; which was that values vary. Different people put different valuations on the same thing. However, in a market place, everyone competing with everyone else adjusts their individual valuations in the light of what competitors are announcing. An example Robbins quoted was a French market place where each seller would "cry aloud" his wares – whereas in less excitable, less Gallic countries they might simply chalk their prices up on a blackboard. I can still hear Lionel Robbins' expressive articulation of the words "cry aloud", ringing in my ears after, as I write, 65 years.

But the point is *communication.* Each seller knows what other sellers announce, and each buyer is able to compare all the offers. Once there is a large enough number of both buyers and sellers, all these economists opined, you have "perfect competition". Well, maybe. A cynic may suspect that nothing in this world is ever perfect! S/he may have a point.

Ever since that period, economists, like naïve young birds have chirruped the same thing, particularly to politicians "Make sure there is perfect competition and the economy will then run at its optimum level". Unfortunately, as Keynes was later to point out, this arrangement does not produce full employment. Perfect competition may fail to give the perfect result! However, be that as it may, all these economists, each in their own country, had successfully warded off Marx's most wicked attack on the social fabric. Not only the rich, but all the middle classes too, could breathe again.

But let me get to the point. All these economists claimed that the price established by perfect competition *was* value.

Wrong. It was just a compromise between different values. It cannot be otherwise. Every buyer would like to pay less; every seller would like to get more, whether competition is perfect or not.

(In making this point, I am altering what I was taught at the L.S.E. in 1947 – 50. But the alteration is not terribly significant. And I would like, *en passant*, to stress to the reader that almost everything else I say in this book was taught then. If any reader finds what I say new or startling, I am driven to wonder if the new generation of economists has perhaps forgotten something?. Aren't they saying the same thing as I say? With very few exceptions, they *should be ....)*

In the American Economic Association's Survey of Contemporary Economics for the year 1950, a book I found most useful in passing my exams in that same year, the point had to be admitted, no American economist had been able to develop a satisfactory economic explanation of the level of *wages.* Wages it was admitted, were determined by the relative strengths of the contending parties i.e. by a *compromise.* Every so often, economic journalists and employers associations will chirrup that "social charges" must be reduced. But they are part, really, of wages. If these charges were abolished, wages would rise by the same amount – that is if what the American Survey said in 1950 remains true.

Marx of course would have disputed the American Association's notion. His theory was that wages had to reflect fairly closely the cost of keeping the worker alive and sufficiently comfortable to be motivated and productive. He may possibly have a point! His argument was based on the idea he had that value was *objective*, not subjective at all, being proportionate, he argued, to the time needed to produce the commodity in question. Now certainly it is quite reasonable for the worker to value his/her time. That is their right. It is what they sell.

But the valuation is just as *subjective* as the employer's valuation of what capital expenditure has been necessitated to give the worker their job. Both values are subjective. Marx's idea was wrongly called a "theory of value". Wrong! It was nothing more than a s*ubjective definition* of value.

So let me restate my understanding of what economics cannot but say about price and value. Quite simply, every price is a compromise between opposing values.

We have a tax called the added value tax. I once argued with the VAT man that there was no value there until I had received the payment for the goods supplied. He replied that the revenue did not take that view. We were both right! The taxpayer is entitled to value only the money received. The tax gatherer is equally entitled to value the goods created. I repeat value is subjective. But I think I can say that perhaps we should call this tax by some other name – but that's just semantics.

So! Value is subjective, OK?

But of course certain groups of people may tend to share similar valuations. I suppose each such group could be regarded as having some sort of separate sub-culture.

"Marketing" is a business philosophy which attempts to discover the consumer valuations of a targeted group. But it still has to effect some sort of *compromise* with the manufacturing company.

"Advertising" tends rather to take the value culture of the producing company for granted and hence studies consumer valuations so as to design campaigns which modify them rather than utilize them.

At one time economists tried to construct a sort of profile of the consumer called "economic man"! This was realistic, perhaps to the extent that limitations of income constrained consumer choice to a significant extent. But this sort of constraint is considerably modified for groups with very high income and may be reduced for all groups in a society with a very high per capita GNP. It will always be constructive to speculate how consumers might behave in various specific situations.

For example, it is a fairly well established fact that when the economy slackens, consumers may adjust their valuation of a new car as against keeping their existing one for (say) another year. Quite a slight slowing down of the overall economy can, for this reason, sometimes produce a totally disproportionate slump in car sales (The problem with the "supply and demand curve" analysis of price determination has always been that the "shape" of the consumer demand curve can change both very rapidly and unpredictably.)

Value, being subjective, nonetheless functions in peoples minds under certain objective constraints. If we seek to spend over and above our income, we incur debts. (The sheer volume of consumer credit attests the strong desire in many people to buy more than they can strictly speaking afford.) But the important thing is to realize that even when consumers limit their purchases to conform with their income, this by no means necessitates any particular distribution of different items in their shopping lists. The value a consumer places on a particular purchase may be very strongly influenced by qualitative factors as much as by the quantitative relationships between price and income. For example, consumers may pay more for an item in a small local shop then in a supermarket – perhaps because they consider the quality better, but also because of a whole host of other factors – difference in opening hours, the fact that a friend or relative works in the shop. They may distrust the supermarket because prices at the till are higher than on the shelf.

Heavy advertizing and the existence of a brand name may persuade consumers to pay more than for an identical generic product.

I could obviously continue! Suffice it to say that human motivation is an extremely complex and subtle matter. Subjective variations in the consumer valuations have considerable influence on prices. What consumers properly value in what they buy is its substance. What advertisers and marketing people value is its image.

What price consumers can be induced to pay is, again, a compromise between the substance and the image. Those who believe that consumers foolishly place too much trust in advertizing can point to the fact that supermarkets can economically sell "own brand" equivalents for less, sometimes quite a bit less than the heavily advertized branded product. I personally believe governments might do well to exploit this fact by putting a tax on advertizing, but I do admit that this would also impact that type of advertizing, sometimes encountered, which does focus on the substance – which can sometimes happen with new products. Of course, even Marx conceded that for a thing to have value, on his definition, it did also have to be *wanted.* The whole purpose of advertizing is to make a thing become wanted – even if it isn't really needed!

This applies to the value of work. Many years ago, I worked for a while as a QWERTY compositor, exploiting the newly arrived photographic or xerographic methods of printing by using what was the called "cold composition". A "qwerty comp" used the typewriter keyboard to produce the typography for book production on hard copy, rather than as hitherto by using lead which has to be melted to make the type. In doing this I found I could easily earn £15 an hour even when I charged lower prices than my competitors. (By quoting lower prices, I had to spend less time than they did canvassing for work, so maybe my income wasn't that much less than theirs.) It was enough to finance my moving to Ireland. But I started getting interested in manufacturing the books as well as doing the type setting for them. This meant I had to do other types of work, and to cost and price these new activities. So, I thought, if I can earn £15 an hour by typesetting, then when I do something else, I am losing £15 an hour – so, therefore, that is my time cost. This is what economists call "opportunity cost". My opportunity cost determined my valuation of my time, *but it was still subjective.* I might have been able "objectively" to get more, but I did not bother to investigate that, because I reasoned, "Let's get started. I may be able to charge more once I have got it going, but I can leave that till later".

But my valuation would still have to compromise with the customer's different valuation. If I guessed right, it was still a guess and a guess is still subjective. Sorry if it is a bit boring to keep stressing this. But you see, while the professors who taught me "implied" strongly that value was subjective, they never got to the point of actually directly saying so! (not unless my memory is gravely at fault!) On the contrary, they seemed to think that the final compromise in setting a price somehow became objective and that the agreed price was in fact the "value"!

I think this is a philosophical error, and moreover an important one because I feel it tends to bedevil arguments over the "right" level of price e.g. of wages. I think the American Association's book in that far off year of 1950 got it right. That I believe is one of the unalterable truths of economics. Marx had called for the abolition of the wages system. Lenin and then Stalin publicly agreed with him. But how it could be abolished not one of the three ever said, and in the Soviet Union they went on paying wages until it collapsed! Moreover, even if the wage system could somehow be abolished, all human beings would still value their work subjectively – because value is an *emotional* matter and we are an emotional species.

However value is "defined", it is only by some arrangement for sharing "added value" that any of us can have any income. Wages, interest, rent, taxes, pension, social security payments, all have this in common; they can only be paid out of the added "value", and this has to be calculated in *money* and *paid in money*. This has implications which should be clearly recognized for the following purposes; -

a) governmental policy regarding employment

b) promoting teamwork in enterprises

c) understanding and "living with" entrepreneurs

d) devising systems by which the added value is to be shared out, or to be used for common purposes.

Note that while it has to be handled in money, only the *real* economy can ***produce*** added value.

Let me recap a little, Exchange tends to take place when buyer and seller place differing valuations on what ever is to be exchanged. But buyer and seller have to be aware of each other, and have to have money in existence unless barter is practicable, which it usually isn't. If they are in different countries, currencies may need to be exchanged. If they are at any distance at all, a suitable mode of effecting payment, such as cheque or credit card may be necessary. Hence it is that we must regard the propensity to exchange, which may be obstructed by all sorts of difficulties, as a *tendency.* Economists have proposed the concept of a "perfect" market as one in which all buyers are in contact with all sellers: but with some notable but limited exceptions in very large cities, most markets are imperfect and some extremely so. There is a sort of *simplistic* economic advice which talks as if all markets were perfect, or nearly so, or perhaps believes they can be made to become so by some administrative action. But such advice needs to be treated with *extreme caution* in the real highly imperfect world!

When an exchange does take place, it has to be understood that the price is a **compromise** between different value systems. Of course, any agreement on price will tend to be copied by others, to the extend they are aware of it, but also to the extent that there are socially agreed value systems in various economically active groups.

Value is (must I keep saying it) entirely subjective. The people who do the work value their labour. The people who want the work done value its usefulness to them. But you can't equate apples and oranges; usefulness and effort *can't* be measured in the *same* units ... Once you see this – and I would have thought it is obvious enough you will surely deduce that no "theory" of value can square this circle. All we can have is different *definitions* of value. Different people all free to define it differently: all one can ask is that in presenting any chain of reasoning, one makes it clear which definition one is using!

For example, Marx's definition of value as "proportionate to labour time" is really quite serviceable, but it is not an obligatory definition: which might be better stated as proportionate to *human* time spent. Personally I see little wrong in his definition of the "price of labour time" as being the "cost of production" of the worker. (Where the debate lies is whether this of itself constitutes "exploitation". Pro-capitalist economists like Jevons and Bohm-Banerk might have responded that it doesn't!)

I think we can accept as reasonably self evident that buyers seek to pay less and sellers to receive more. But when economists seek to go further and seek to establish **where** the compromise should be and **how** it can be calculated we are already into the realm of debate.

A fellow student at college, who had been in the war and hence was a mature student, went into his first lectures in the theory of pricing. He related what he had been told to a friend who was in business. The friend listened. When the student had finished, the businessman glanced at his watch and said "Come, the pubs are open now, I'll buy you a drink". (In those far off days one could not drink in London pub before 5pm). And all the debate then focused on the word "value".

If one could establish the value of a commodity, one could then reason that the compromise between buyer and seller *could* be at that value, and perhaps should be there, by an extension of reasoning

The Oxford Concise dictionary lists 9 different meanings of the noun "value". Only a few of these meanings can be measured objectively. All the others are subjective, except in so far as they express the amount of some price – but one cannot explain price by price! Wahrig's Worderbuch similarly lists two main meanings – Gettung, Bedeutung, Wichtigkeit and Preis, ... den man beim Verkauf bekommen wurde – of which the first is subjective and the second again begs the question. For "valeur", Larousse gives10 meanings, two of which could be seen as objective. The Irish *An Fodoir Beag* lists 4 meanings for "luach", all quantitative. Finally the European Union long ago accepted the French tax on added value, but defines value as what is left by the prices actually paid for purchases subtracted from the prices actually received from sales. (In England I was once told that the Revenue held that this applied even when, because of a bad debt, nothing had been received from sales.)

I conclude that for economic analysis there is no level of "value" which can be *objectively* determined as opposed to actual price. The American Economic Association's *Survey of Contemporary Economics* in 1950 reported the effect that no American economist had at that time proposed any *viable* analysis for the determination of wage levels beyond the "respective strengths" of employers and unions: this meant no value could be objectively attributed to "labour". Of course, economists do propound "theories" of value, but I submit that all they are doing is to express various possible **definitions** of value. They can use these definitions in their own set of propositions, but any conclusions they draw are thus *conditional.*

It has been said by no less a speaker than Jesus Christ that one cannot worship both God and Mammon. If this dictum were applied to economies, it would call into question the way in which we treat money! There can be detected, particularly in the financial sector of the economy, a tendency to put money on a sort of pedestal, as if it measured value. It doesn't. Much economic debate currently seems to be between a financial sector which argues that if the "real" economy would only behave "better", there would be no problems – and a "real" sector which has to argue the exact opposite ...

The whole question of value is fraught with contradictions. When Marx and Hegel met in the Elysian Fields, no doubt Marx said to Hegel that there was "contradiction" in capitalism. And I imagine Hegel replied that of course there was, because there was contradiction in everything. At this point I can imagine Heracleitos interjecting that while Hegel was right, contradictions between opposites could be settled by the Logos, by reason.

There is a contradiction certainly, between the way we join together to create added "value" and the way we then argue about how much each of us is to get out of it. None of the various "syntheses" – the entrepreneurial, the Marxist, or the less well-known anthroposophist one – really resolve this contradiction. Maybe it never will be resolved: we'll have, I suppose, to see. We can merely look at where in practice we are, and give a rough account of it, but we have to bear in mind the inherent philosophical limitations of that account. (Perhaps economics is really an impossible discipline.)

Unless added value is enough to pay the people in the business enough to live on, clearly they would starve, unless kept alive by charity ... or benefits of some kind. When added value is more than enough for the people in the business to live on, a surplus is created. This may be used in various ways;

a) It can be shared amongst the people in the business: there needs to be some agreement as to how it should be distributed.

b) It can be used to expand the business in what ever way seems desirable.

c) Some of it will be demanded by the government in taxes,

But whatever happens as to all this, it will still be based on compromise between different valuations.

It is perhaps pertinent to mention the distinction made by my teachers at LSE in 1947/50 between what they called micro and macro economics. The former dealt with the "theory of the firm" and the latter with "national income". But I think the distinction is only necessary if we are trying to resolve competing "theories" of value. Once we accept that there can be no such thing as an *objective* theory of a *subjective* notion, we can then let different **definitions** of value co-exist side by side, used for different purposes. The reason for the definition of macro economic was that practicing economists have to look at statistics which have perforce to be collected in money terms. Non-monetary statistics can't be correlated! When Volkswagen had produced its millionth Beetle, it assembled a lot of them in its carpark, and by arranging ones with darker paintwork in a pile of ones with lighter paintwork, it was able to spell out the words "EINE MILLIONEN" and photograph this from the air. But why it made an effective publicity stunt was that everyone knew what one VW was really worth! Without that social appraisal, a Visitor from outer space, descending towards that carpark would (even if he could somehow read German) have muttered to himself "So what?"

Only the *value* of production has meaning. If national production statistics have to be in money, my teachers 60 odd years ago were uneasily aware that they were teaching that money only roughly represented value. So they coined the term "macro economics" to dodge away from the theoretical problem! In the macro, maybe one could forget what one said when lecturing about the micro? (!)

Incidentally about this time, a Polish economist Hilary Minc (pronounced Mints I think) analyzed Polish national income statistics in the terminology of Marx. He broke down the Polish national income into "c + u +s"; "c" equalled purchases plus depreciation, "u" equalled wages and "s" the "surplus value". I dont know what happened to Minc. I hope he didn't get purged! Because his work must have been deeply embarrassing! It surely suggested that the communist regime was continuing "exploitation".

Value is subjective. Oh dear, I've said it yet again! But that's why Minc's work was, I have to say it nonsense ...Think about that dear reader.

5. THE ENTREPRENEUR

I myself have switched from being a consultant to being an entrepreneur. I find the consultancy background a *disadvantage. I'd take too long making decisions!* I spent too much time either analyzing situations or defending my decisions to other people. I found I had to stop analyzing and instead take decisions *instinctively*, And if need be, to say to critics, "well maybe you're right - **but this is how I do it.** " And if the critics persisted, all I could add was "well, we'll see".

It seems to me that this is why entrepreneurs ought to be *absolute owners:* only that way can they get on with implementing their *sna*p decisions. (Which is why *all* regulations are inherently wrong?) Every human life is an experiment; the entrepreneur can be no exception.

An entrepreneur is a single unique person. S/he must follow their own vision, which is *almost by definition* different from that of anyone else's. (Could there be such a thing as a group entrepreneur?)

He should only use his own money. He should work hard and save to make a start rather than borrow. *If his vison is valid, it will be self-financing.* (Adam Smith was very clear about this - he was *agains*t limited share companies, for this very reason) This makes an entrepreneur a difficult person to get on with. In my view there is a "cultural" problem here, which we have yet to address. Perhaps we never will.

A new entrepreneur starting a new business has first to *imagine* it. So *imagination* may be his key quality. If at any time we dont have enough entrepreneurs we should perhaps check out whether there are any current cultural influences which tend to restrict or diminish the imagination.

Does television sap the imagination? Social psychologists, please investigate. Of course, imagination by itself won't be enough. The entrepreneur must also think things through. This is not necessarily an exercise in financial prophesy. Any new entrepreneur must realize that s/he is taking *a risk* – and not only that, but that the risk is not easily quantifiable.. Nor can market research help him much. One can only do market research into *known* products. New enterprise is likely to involve either new products or new customers as well ...

A new business is venturing into the unknown, "boldly going where no man has gone before!" *Established business cannot do this sort of thing.* Their shareholders and their bankers will demand that they avoid risk! Who is going to let other people risk their money? *The genuine entrepreneur is going to have to risk his own money.* So it is rather misguided to imagine that new entrepreneurs can have much use for "stock" banking or "how –to-do it advice.

A new business idea is *axiomatically* risky because, being new, it has not been tried before. So an **entrepreneur**

1) has an idea and a **new** one at that

2) is prepared to risk **his own money.**

3) has **imagination.**

NB In taking risks he has the **chance** of making profit: but not all entrepreneurs are driven by a mere desire to make money.

So an entrepreneur must back his own judgment, often going against notions, "informed" or "established". In forming his judgment, he may be acting on nothing other than a hunch. If it's right, he will be successful. If it's wrong he won't be. There must be many unsuccessful entrepreneurs to "produce" one successful one! Unless everything is tried, no one can know for sure what really succeeds. *The economy develops by trial and error;* if there were no entrepreneurs, what would ever get tried out? Maybe if there were no entrepreneurs, there would be fewer errors; but there would be no real development. The universe is continually changing! Without entrepreneurs, how can the economy ever adapt to change?

(The astute reader may wonder, if this is true, how can Eurocrats sitting in their ivory tower in Brussels, determine in advance exactly what any entrepreneur is allowed to do ? I suggest that astute reader asks them. I hope s/he can elicit an answer from them ...)

The CEO of a large corporation is unlikely to be an entrepreneur. Even if he had the right qualities, the terms of his engagement would prevent him from using them. Of course such large companies can coast on for many years - on the initial impetus of their founding entrepreneur ... Note that an entrepreneur does not have to be rich before he starts. Marks and Spencer's started from a market stall ... The entrepreneur functions *ex ante.*

He imagines a future business, before he sets to work creating it. He doesn't tell anyone his thought processes. He will be wary of saying anything at all about his plans. He does not want to give his ideas away to competitors. In short, what the entrepreneur does is *qualitative*.

In a "classic" slump businesses used to go bankrupt: so in a "classic" boom, new businesses used to take their place. At least that's how it was in the Victorian age – before oligopoly raised its ugly head. When there was a recovery, we only noticed the work of entrepreneurs *ex post.* We cannot forecast their achievements.

A couple of years ago no less a person than HM the Queen asked why no-one foresaw the crisis. Maybe the crisis was caused by a dearth of new entrepreneurs? Today's true entrepreneurs may be operating in the black economy. Or they may be Mafiosi, or money launderers. Not only do we not know. It is questionable whether we can discover a means of finding out! We can and do ask existing businesses what they intend doing .But we cannot ask *new* entrepreneurs such a question, because we do not yet know who they are. This of course plays havoc with all the gubbins of econometric forecasting which, axiomatically, can only deal with numbers and can only manipulate *ex post* facts. The entrepreneur may be temperamentally impervious to numbers! His success or failure in an uncertain world may simply be due to luck, good or bad. His much-vaunted belief in himself may be totally irrational. He may be more like a stupid bull in a china shop than a careful or cautious calculator.

Not only does he take risks in external uncertainty. He himself is internally uncertain.

If entrepreneurs are business persons with **new** ideas, such ideas can only be expressed in a language. Different countries have different languages, and the development of ideas in any country inevitably has a "flavour" attributable to that country's language and the historical processes in which the national ideas have been debated. It seems to me that it is therefore rather likely that new entrepreneurs will not necessarily appear in all countries in equal numbers at the same time. Europe is suffering from a *shortage* of new entrepreneurs – that is why, as I write, we still have rising Eurozone unemployment. But I suspect the shortage will be worse in some EU countries than in others ...

It seems to me important to note that an entrepreneur may well function not on a single idea, but on a whole complex of related ideas. This was certainly the case with Henry Ford. Changing from individually crafted cars to mass produced ones required in his view

1) Assembly line production

2) Machinery specially designed

3) A different system of labour relations

4) Careful management of the use of outside suppliers so that the line was not stopped because of some non-arrival of essential components.

5) As far as possible production of components within the factory (For this reason Ford's plant at Dagenham once contained a blast furnace, the only one in the South of England)

6) Continual analysis of the whole production process to locate cost reductions (eg by substituting stampings for castings)

7) A doctrine of how society should be.

An entrepreneur can only start up when hitherto unrelated ideas are brought together and when all the basic ideas are systematically thought through. To the extent that is so, our contemporary "snippet-culture" may be detrimental to entrepreneurship. An entrepreneur may get further from reading one book right through and thoroughly digesting, it than by looking at lots of paragraphs from different books. And if his mind works by analogy or metaphor, that one book might be a novel or whatever! It might be the case that his one book might be selected quite by chance. *We do not know.* Because we do not know how inspiration works...

But no modern industrial society can function without entrepreneurs. This is why Soviet Communism failed, once it abandoned the New Economic Policy of Lenin and Stalin, which farmed state industry out to them. It may also be why Chinese communism (as I write) is the fastest growing economy in the world , faster even than Turkey, Russia, India or Brazil – because they let entrepreneurs get on with it. We will always have to have entrepreneurs. At present we will have different categories of people at work: -

- entrepreneurs
- managers
- supervisors
- workers
- small businessmen/women,

who can only adjust their competing claims by compromise. This is why democracy is probably as Churchill put it, "the worst of all possible systems except for all the others". It is *workable* because the members of each category are probably more likely to accept existing compromises, if they feel they can in time be renegotiated. *"Command systems" cannot do this.* Unlike CEOs, entrepreneurs are not much obsessed with reducing wage costs and headcounts. Henry Ford believed in a high wage economy. Maybe he had a point.

Recap

1) Only entrepreneurs can make the economy zip. (Read Adam Smith or at least what Arthur Herman says about him in his brilliant book, *The Scottish Enlightenment.*)

2) Bureaucrats can **stifle** new entrepreneurs, though they'll probably get round this.

3) Politicians shouldn't rely on advice from old entrepreneurs, because

a) they become ossified with age

b) they seldom understand economics – they work by the seat of their pants.

4) Take it from me, as a business economist, and consultant, with *well over half a century's experience* – a healthy economy needs a continual flow of new entrepreneurs. *Let me stress the word "new"!*

Old entrepreneurs in fact strive to prevent young entrepreneurs competing with them. The trouble is they get politicians to help them! (Politicians are easily fooled by entrepreneurs, who are skilled at presenting their self-interest as if it were economic wisdom.) We *need* entrepreneurs. But, bluntly, we need the young new ones more than the old established ones. So we must prevent old entrepreneurs from getting legislation and regulations drafted in their interests. For this reason, **don't** vote for politicians who hob-nob with old entrepreneurs! Except by getting back to old-fashioned laissez-faire, we dont need to encourage entrepreneurs. If they need much encouragement, they are not entrepreneurs.

If you should want to read a "case study" which can support your understanding of all this, why not look at Susanna Hoe's book *The Man Who Gave His Company Away.* This is about Ernest Bader, the founder of Scott Bader, the reinforced fibre glass plastics people. As Schumacher remarks in his introduction, Bader was an archetypal entrepreneur; and as Christopher Budd, the anthropological economist believes, in economics, once you understand the archetype, you know all you need to know. I think there may be lot of truth in this view.

I only knew Ernest Bader in his old age, when he very generously funded my translation of Wilken's *Capital,* but from Susanna Hoe's book, I did get a picture of how he must have been in his dynamic entrepreneurial youth – which, incidentally, was before he developed his radical ideas on company ownership. I am not sure that Bader's successors would want him brought back to life. He was probably rather difficult to live with. I do know that when we had a little "talk-in" on Wilken's book at Scott Baders's premises in Northamptonshire, I tactlessly let slip a remark about the role of the entrepreneurs in business. It went down like a lead balloon. But you see, this is probably because the Scott Bader company has passed on from the first stage of rapid growth. So there would be little point in trying to find another entrepreneur to succeed him.

This problem was dramatically dealt with in Shaw's stimulating play "Major Barbara". Do read it! Andrew Undershaft, the entrepreneur in this play, runs a large company whose founder decreed that in each generation it should be left to a foundling. In the play it turns out that Barbara's fiancée is technically a foundling and so inherits the company - a huge joke because he is hardly the entrepreneurial type, you may think. But who knows: it might have worked ...

Entrepreneurs in real life probably can't find another entrepreneur to succeed them. Hence it is that companies tend to pass through a life cycle, in which three distinct phases can ensue: let me repeat:-

a) First phase; creation and growth of the company by its entrepreneur

b) Second phase: on the death or retirement of the entrepreneur, he is succeeded by a team of managers; these may have the skills needed to keep the company in business, but may lack the often somewhat irrational determination of the real entrepreneur

c) The original entrepreneur's capital idea becomes superseded by changing technologies and changing markets, and unless a new entrepreneur can be found, begins to run down. It is necessary to understand clearly that any new entrepreneur must either already be a most substantial shareholder or must become such. A manager who is only putting his shareholders' money at risk cannot be a real entrepreneur. A substantial shareholder who has the imagination and drive to put all necessary changes into effect can perhaps become an entrepreneur, but will probably need to effect more radical alterations than are likely to get support of less involved and less committed shareholders. How long this life cycle can take depends very much on market and technological circumstances.

It should be noted that even the most determined new entrepreneur must fairly quickly achieve a sufficient return of capital employed to avoid spending his own money beyond the point of no return. However this situation might conceivably change. The next global stock market collapse, when it comes, will make 1929 seem like a tea party. With all the modern technological aids, it will come very quickly indeed. And just as 1929 was, it will be totally unexpected.

Not totally unexpected in 1929. The journalist Claud Cockburn recalled in his autobiographical notes, (*In Time of Trouble, London 1957)* how the expert stock market analyst of the day, Louis Hinrichs' stopped in a disconcerting manner he had, when he wanted to make an important point, and spreading his fingers in the fluttering motion which expressed uneasiness and certain bewilderment , he said

"All the same, Claud, I don't believe it" In New York at that moment there was only one "it" of which you could say that (op.cit, p147)

And that "it" was the belief, eerily familiar today, that " the whole world was going to get happy by getting richer and richer. It would start of course with people who were gambling in American stocks getting rich, and then the rest of the Americans would become prosperous too, and pretty soon the whole world. America felt kindly towards the world that summer - - when it had a moment to think of it all. In any case, there was no need to think of it much, because America was going to solve all the world's problems automatically " (op.cit, p 145)

Cockburn was of course a communist, but Hinrichs wasn't anything of the sort, on the contrary he believed the capitalist way to be the only way. We do not, as I write, have the same sense of quite manic over-confidence. I dont myself find that too reassuring though.

We do, notably in Europe, have an *idée fixe* that we have found the one right way forward.

We haven't.

There is *no* one right way forward. As change ensues all sorts of unexpected events may shatter our present credo. We may then have to look for other ways, and we may have to just try them out and see what happens. But if there were another, vaster 1929, it would enable rich people to buy up and completely own derelict companies with some sort of assets. Some of these rich people might, you never know, become "repeat" entrepreneurs . It cannot be ruled out.

Could anyone become an entrepreneur? Most people in a developed society with a reasonably high GNP per head could save enough to start up on their own. All they need is a "capital" idea. An economy with a larger number of small firms might be more efficient and might adopt more rapidly to change. More people starting up on their own might possibly reduce unemployment, so perhaps more useful work would be done. For many people to do this does seem to require a somewhat more business-oriented "culture" in society. Entrepreneurs can and do challenge wrong cultures. In this they are sometimes helped, surprisingly perhaps, by authors. This is because literature thrives on imagination. I thought it worthwhile to republish a Marxist (!) philosopher's studies of literary matters, and have slanted my promotion of it as being about an *entrepreneurial* culture ... I rather hope some new entrepreneur might read it. Well you never know ...

6. THE DIVERGENCE OF MONEY

Once I was on holiday in the Lleyn Peninsula. A Welsh speaking local was passing by the cottage we were staying in. We talked for a while. "Money iss funny things" he said, using a local pronunciation of English. He was right.

This is because money is "secondary" to the real economy. So "secondary" that when I was at the London School of Economics in 1947 – 50, it was taught as a "separate" subject with different lecturers and different text books. I cannot recall that it was ever explained why this was done. I think it just seemed to be a matter of convenience. And it must be remembered that the English attitude to philosophy is rather pragmatic in tendency

So when that awful continental iconoclast Marx had to be gently abutted, one aspect of the abuttal, in England, at any rate, was to draw economics away from too close a connection with philosophy, seen as a quite *separate* discipline ... But this did mean that one implication of the *subjectivity* of value was, I think somewhat overlooked.

If "price" results from the encounter between the noticeably different valuations of buyers and sellers, then price is not and cannot be "objective". It can only be a *compromise* between these diverging valuations. Now the total of all the prices in the economy at any point of time gives you the amount of money in use at that point. Keep that in mind, dear reader, keep it always in mind.

Because, do you see, the corollary must therefore be that the amount of money (called the "supply" of money) is the *product* of a vast series of tiny little compromises of millions of people in millions of mostly very small transactions, all over the whole country, on any given day.

Thus it is not the "supply" of money which determines prices, *its t'other way round!* We are stuck with the term "supply of money" but isn't it something of a misnomer. What is really happening is that the individual transactions produce a vast supply of prices *to which money must conform.*

Whatever amount of money is lying around, whether in strongrooms, bank accounts, pockets and purses (or simply in a cardboard box under Grandma's bed), an amount so very big and so practically impossible to calculate – what ever that amount is, it is today's total of transactions that determine how much of that amount is actually going to be used today. Got it? It is a little difficult to get one's head round it all, is it not? But that is how it is. Bear that in mind always.

You see, if valuations are *subjective* and so vary between each individual and the next, the vast total of all the goods of every conceivable kind on offer every day is *objective*. It is a vast and extraordinarily complex *fact* that today quite definitely and (theoretically) countable amounts of each and every commodity are on sale. That is what the real economy does. Every day it produces a simply astronomical number of commodities. Everyday some of these may be bought, and the rest left till tomorrow, but that they are *there* today is objective fact. But you cannot add apples and oranges. Only by their *prices* can they be added together into the whole economy. But that adding together is simply something government statisticians have to do *in their mind.* Because all they are doing is adding up prices which are only compromises between different subjective valuations. "Money iss funny things". A pearl of Celtic wisdom!

The real economy has done, each day, a gigantic task of *real* production for sale. Fundamentally subjective valuations of each separate item in this colossal mountain of supplies produce the so-called supply of money. It seems to me adequate to say, therefore, that the real economy is primary and its money reflection is secondary. It cannot possibly be the other way round, can it?

If you look in the mirror before leaving the house in the morning, you may notice an egg stain on your chin. You can't remove that stain by rubbing the mirror with a damp cloth! Defects in the real economy cannot easily be corrected the way governments seem to think, by their tinkering with money. The whole burden of economic theory is that in a free market, buyers will use money to send signals to sellers to correct anything buyers think is wrong. Today's signals are too late to affect *today's* supplies. They can only affect future supplies, and then only at a time lag. Buyers find today's prices for eggs a bit high. So they may buy tomatoes instead, for tomorrow's breakfast. That sends a signal to egg producers – fewer eggs were sold today than normal. Eggs go off. They'd probably do best to lower their prices. That is how market events send signals.

Over the whole economy, can I switch to another analogy? The money economy is like a *garment* for the real economy. It isn't necessarily a good fit. If monetary affairs are badly managed, it may fit "only where it touches" ...

The divergence between the real economy and money is fundamental, but it varies in extent from time to time and from sector to sector, and from place to place. In this chapter, in attempting to explain this divergence, I will have to dart about in what is likely to seem a rather haphazard fashion. I don't know if that can be helped. Sorry!

The divergence between real economy and money was extraordinarily wide in the German "run-away" inflation of the early 1920s. I had my very first lesson in economics at the age of eight, when the next-door neighbour, who'd been in Germany at the time, gave me a 500 million mark note to play with!

At college, we studied the "theory of the firm": abstract, but logical enough. But until I got my second job as a business economist in March 1960 I had no more idea than the man in the moon of how a real large industrial company was run. Money of course came into it – but in what way?

I was recruited by John Barber, later to be Ford of England's Director of Finance, but then Controller. At that far-off time, Dagenham was run almost as if it were an independent company. It wasn't really, but it did look as if it were because

a) there was a minority holding by English shareholders and so the company was quoted on the London Stock Exchange

b) it had accumulated some £60 million (then a very large sum indeed) from accumulated profits.

The post- war boom was still then continuing. *These profits could not be remitted to America because there were then very rigorous exchange controls!*

c) it had its own models, very different from the American ones

d) it was supplied by British firms, and, true to Ford ideas, had its own blast furnace and foundry.

c) it was the largest overseas subsidiary of the American parent company in Dearborn, Detroit.

So what you may say? Well, much of this separateness was possibly due to the "economic nationalism" of the 1930s, when Dagenham was founded. After the world collapse of 1929, each industrial country had erected tariff walls, which prevented the importation of manufactured goods from other countries. Neither goods nor money could move freely about the world. Otherwise Ford could well have made all its cars in America and shipped them to England. The shape of world industry was being decisively affected by the 1929 collapse of the money economy and its aftermath. It even looked as if money was primary and the real economy secondary! Only in the 1960s and 1970s did the primary nature of the real world economy begin again to assert itself. I happen to believe that will always happen.

By 1960, Henry Ford was beginning to get really restive about the British maintenance of this monetary straight-jacket around a real economic unit. The parent company had nearly gone bankrupt, yet the profitable English company's resources were unavailable to it! The English establishment saw nothing wrong in this! Economic nationalism still prevailed. They saw Dagenham as an *English* business which just happened to be partly American owned. They were wrong.

I found that Ford Dagenham was run by its engineers. They designed the cars. Their designs were getting very much better. The Mark II Zephyr was far better than the Mark I. The Anglia was better than the Popular. Note the name "Anglia"! Because the cars were good and getting better, obviously there would be a profit. I didn't at first understand this. I had been trained in the *academic* "theory of the firm". By this theory, entrepreneurs were financial calculating machines. They started with money. They were already rich, they built a factory, any factory would do and paid wages to workers who would produce whatever it was: and because they were money motivated, it would make a profit. Profit was the reward rich people got for not spending all their money on themselves.

When John Barber briefed me on my first day at work, he did think to tell me I would find it all "very strange". I didn't say so, but I was *puzzled* by all this. Here was a company with a sophisticated Finance staff. Surely it was axiomatic that Finance would run the business? It didn't. (Shouldn't I have been told that that was how it was, at college? I wasn't!) But it happened that there was a new situation, which made me believe (for the first few weeks) that all I had to do was to apply the "theory of the firm" in practice. *I still thought the money economy was primary!*

What had happened was simple enough, American Ford, instead of going bankrupt, has been turned round. There may have been earlier cases of this happening, I don't know. If American Ford had been owned by *unengaged* shareholders, they'd have sold out to Chrysler or General Motors. That's how the money economy works, usually. *But Henry Ford had his name on the building.* (He was the second HF, not the first) He had no intention of selling out. Nor was there any need to, really. He brought in the famous Harvard "whizz-kids". He gave them the task of re-shaping the company, so as to save it. So things did look quite like the "theory of the firm". But it wasn't really so. The near bankruptcy had been caused by the failure of an important new model to sell. This was scrapped, and better new models, more in line with changing American tastes, were designed, and proved to be OK. Of course for a while, money was very tight. So a system was set up which *vetted* all projects, to check that they would earn a target "return on assets employed".

But all this really meant was that projects were to be financially **inspected** closely. But they were not decided on for financial reasons. The inspection of an ex-ante target return of assets depended absolutely on *ex-ante* target sales forecasts! Really, all that was happening was the company was being a little bit more careful about money, When you nearly go bankrupt, you have to be!

Probably most large companies under capitalism have always been run by the engineers. I dont know. It is perhaps something that economic historians should study. Certainly since the industrial revolution started, innovative engineers have made continual and often dramatic improvements in productivity. Productivity determines the size of the cake. It does not determine how the cake is cut up between owner, engineers and workers. Rolt's famous biography of Brunel tends to plead that he, the great engineer, did not get a fair share. But that is a value judgment, and so outside the proper subject matter of economics.

What is clear enough is that if the technology was successful, the company would be profitable. Decisions about the future were arrived at by developing test prototypes, not by monetary forecasts. The doyen of the "whizz-kids" was Robert MacNamara, later to be Kennedy's Secretary of State. He certainly did set up a new and sophisticated financial *inspection* system. This had got to Dagenham, not all that long before I was recruited. By the time I arrived this was well under way. Dagenham boasted an expanding "Central Finance" function, divided into departments for financial analysis, financial planning and financial control ("control" meant what it means in French – "inspection".) New projects – setting up a new plant, developing a new model – *had to show that they would earn a target return on assets employed.* The English Ford engineers took little notice. Why should they. The mark II Zephyrs were doing well. (Lovely cars - I wish I still had one.)

But then there was a confrontation. Hitherto, models in the States and Britain had been totally different. But now Dearborn had developed a projected *small car!* Dagenham was now *competing* with Dearborn! The Cortina was then a project. We had to prepare a "submission" to the great man. There was to be a slide projection in a darkened room at Dearborn. The proposed new model, its technical details, its styling *and its financial projections!* It must be understood that Dearborn was far from delighted with Dagenham's competition! Why should the Ford empire develop two new small cars *when one would do*?

Only because of those wretched exchange controls. Profits could not be sent back to America. But they could be spent in England - for example on developing a new model. The Bank of England could not let such a large sum of money leave the sterling area. It might even precipitate devaluation. So Henry Ford had to grin and bear it; two similar small cars instead of one. This was too much really. Money considerations were screwing the real economy up. Something would have to be done. The accumulated Ford profits had swollen to £60 million – then an **enormous** sum. So that you can gauge it, let me tell you that English Ford directors were paid an average of £20,000 a year each. That sounds tiny now, but of course the value of money has plummeted since then. I was living comfortably in a detached house, modernizing the kitchen, *and* running an overdrive Zephyr on I think it was £1300 a year. So £60 million was really *enormous!* Henry Ford wanted it back – but couldn't get hold of it.

This produced a professionally interesting situation for me! At LSE I had learnt about the London money market *in theory*. Now, in the open-plan office, at the desk next to mine was a colleague who was actually *playing* this money market! His name was Bert Dennett. I think he played it well. Every day he would move parts of the £60 million from one short-term government security to another. I have never seen a man enjoy his job so much as Bert did – he had a whale of a time... But as I say, Henry Ford was very tense. He first bought out the minority shareholding on the London Stock Exchange. Questions were asked by Labour MPs, in the House of Commons. (This of course reduced English Ford's purely notional "independence". But Henry Ford didn't see why he should share Dagenham profits with others.

He could now dispense with this bit of outside finance. He didn't need it any more, and what was more to the point he didn't *want* it. *The real economy is made up by what everyone in the country or countries concerned wants.* Of course, wealthy people find it easier to get what they want!

The Tory government saw no objection to the share deal, so that at least was allowed. The saga of the £60 million was to continue. I worked for a while in Alan Shepherd's department (He was later to run Grand Metropolitan Hotels). We often worked into the small hours of the morning. We went through the Stock Exchange yearbook looking for a large company that would be worth £60 million. Our final idea was to buy up Massey-Ferguson, the Canadian tractor company. In the end the money was used to set up a hire-purchase company, a sales-oriented scheme. I suppose the engineers thought that Ford tractors were better than Massey-Ferguson.

Of course, English Ford engineers did have to go through the motions of the new financial inspection. If each project has, *ex ante*, to claim it will achieve the target return on assets employed, then the total assets of the company – the land, buildings and ancillary services had to be **apportioned** among the various projects. I'd been there a few weeks and I was asked to devise a formula for this apportionment. So I recalled the "theory of the firm"! I worked on a formula based on the floor space each project would occupy. My scheme was unceremoniously rejected. I was a bit hurt by this. But the departmental head who threw it out was an *accountant*. I learnt for the first time that accountants and economists seldom see eye to eye. Accountants only work *ex post* , and avoid approximations.

That a rough approximation would be adequate *ex ante* was an unacceptable notion. My scheme was too "theoretical". Even when money really should moderate what's *real*, it often has a hard job with *real* managers.

But I am digressing. Let me get back to a hushed darkened room in Dearborn, with the Cortina project being run through on the slide projector. It came to the forward financial projections. *Henry Ford got up.* He said *"I'm not satisfied with the forward profits" and walked out.* John Barber managed to get him to agree to a "revision", to be shown to Henry as quickly as possible. I imagine this was caused by Henry Ford's *impatience* with the British involvement. As soon as De Gaulle banned Britain from joining the Common Market, Henry Ford started switching his new money from Dagenham to Ford Köln

But this too was not only motivated by money, although De Gaulle's ban did damage Dagenham's profitability in the short run. *Other forces were also at work* Let me explain. My last job before leaving Ford to move into management consultancy was to rebut a study by a Dearborn economist. It purported to show that productivity in England was lower than productivity in Germany. *This was actually not so.*

It was moreover *irrelevant!* Motor industry productivity was and still is determined by *technology*. A plant of a given size *anywhere in the world* would have the *same* output per man-hour worked! National "characteristics" simply did not come into it at all. But of course that was not a *sufficient* argument for me to act as advocate in the prevailing Dagenham/Dearborn struggle! I was however able to show that both in the motor industry overall, and in manufacturing generally, productivity was in fact higher in Britain than in Germany. I also found that while Volkswagen did have higher productivity than Dagenham, this was because at that time they only made the one model, the Beetle, and so had quite *phenomenal* economies of scale. But there was then a long string of smaller German car companies, some of which were very small indeed – and so had low productivity. In the motor industry productivity goes with size. So Germany's average was lower than Britain's. Some Dagenham directors were quite taken with my study. But things had gone too far for them to be able to do much with it. Many of us left, myself included. Alan Shepherd went to another British car company, John Barber became finance director of A.E.I. and I believe he would have turned it round, but un-engaged shareholders didn't want to wait and sold out to G.E.C. over his head. I then hoped other companies would be interested in applying the Ford financial system: but if there were any such I couldn't locate them and so I moved into management education for a few years. "Management" is, in my view, really applied *real* economics. Those who think economics is only about money won't agree, of course. That is how the divergence affects our thinking

What do these somewhat random events show us? At college my teachers were very much against practical examples! As they saw it, what they had to inculcate was the pure logic of economic reasoning, the logos of work, which cannot change, unless there is a second coming! I suspect their attitude was however partly based on this somewhat artificial division of economics into *two* "subjects", when it is really only *one.* I think practical examples help us to trace the diverse ramifications of the divergence between the real economy and its money reflection. This divergence is sharper in some places than in others, and must vary in different periods and conjectural situations. The money garment only fits the real economy where it touches.

I would advise anyone who wishes to take what I say further, to look for examples of all sorts and analyze them, *with particular regard to this divergence.* The real economy is composed of what everyone wants, but everyone wants different things. Henry Ford wanted one thing: the Governor of the Bank of England another. Was Al Baume wanting to see Germany favoured because he had German ancestry? Or maybe he had that distrust of the "Limey's" that is something found in mid-western Americans? I never actually met him, so I've no idea. Had we ever discussed things, he might well have thought that, far from him being the one with some national prejudice, it was I who was desperately trying to keep England on top as against Germany. I'd have had to admit there might be some truth in this. But both of us, being economists, would have at least gone to the facts and the economic analysis of the facts. *Most of the 7000 million actors in the world economy do no such thing!* Might it be better if more of them did?

Be that as it may, the real economy is a *living thing,* striving for its *future*. By contrast the money economy is concerned only with totting up, *ex post,* money results of the *past.* To the money economy, the future is merely an extrapolation. Was the advent of financial control at Fords in some way a switch from the real to the money economy? I think not. It was an intelligent response to a new situation. What management has to do is to set targets, measure performance against them, devise remedies for shortfalls, and persuade people to adopt the remedies. This is certainly how MacNamara saw it. I happened to see a Churchillian memo to Dagenham from the great Robert MacNamara. It asked briefly, was Dagenham yet using a new report form he had devised? And if not **how were they managing without it?**

That's to do with controlling *performance* – not so much the money reflection of performance – its "management" of it. What had happened was that technology by itself had not ensured survival. I dont know how much MacNamara was moved by money. He was reputed to be a quiet, puritanical man, whose relaxation was to go into the countryside. I can't easily imagine him spending $17,000 on his daughters birthday party, as Henry Ford was supposed to have done around this time.

Even more puritanical were the Russian managers in the "idealistic" phase of early Soviet growth, in the 1930s. Apparently they boasted of taking home *less pay* than the shop floor workers! The managerial class was however growing rapidly, during the Russian Wirtschaftswunder. The construction of the Moscow underground was undertaken precisely so that the new elite could all have nice houses in the suburbs ...

Again what was De Gaulle's motivation when he vetoed British Entry? Was it that Citroen and Renault didn't want Cortinas flooding into France? They were going to get Volkswagens anyway, because of some long-past row De Gaulle had had with Churchill during the war. Or was it simply a shrewd political appraisal that the British would never be happy in a **directive-run** command economy in the Continental style. Nor are they!

The point is, the real economy consist of *people* – living, eating and drinking, having affairs outside their marriages, involved in bitter political conflicts, etc, etc, etc.. The 19th century notion of "economic man" does not exist and surely *cannot* exist. Most people do most of the things they do for quite other reasons: their deeds do have economic *consequences* ... but these are incidental. All the money economy does is to tell us the *results,* ex post. Money is only there because of the "division of labour". Money is needed to facilitate ways in which the net product can be shared out.

Money cannot do anything to see that it is shared out *fairly*. If top managers use their power to pay themselves million pound bonuses that is because of money system deficiencies. Is there any *real-economy* need for these bonuses? Money can tell us when the real economy is faltering, but it may not be able to tell us **why!** If the monetary system is badly managed that can make the economy falter. Monetary management *ought* to be about seeing that that never happens. Note that the banking system has its <u>own</u> interests, just like any other *sector* of the economy has. If banking interests are given excessive priority over other interests, there will be problems. The economy has to make sensible working compromises between various interests.

Don't think that the real economy can be brought under the control of the money mirror of it! Not even by the work of accountants, can that happen. Why companies are obliged to have accountants is because of the tax inspector. Their role is *not* to reveal what the real economy is doing! On the contrary, they are paid to *disguise* what is really happening if they can. The same is true for the shareholders, at least for the vast mass of ordinary shareholders who are effectively in a minority, even when they seem to be the majority – simply because it isn't easy for shareholders to act together. What such shareholders are really doing is *lending* money to the people who actually run things, largely for themselves. Where there are neither tax inspectors nor shareholders there is little need for accounting. Henry Ford used to look at administrative overheads not through budgetary figures, but through the white-collar *headcount.*

If he was of the opinion that Parkinson's Law was at work, he would simply instruct that the headcount be *reduced.* (The same might be done with the swollen civil service today!) Proof that without tax or shares, accounting gets *minimized* could be found in Brussels. As far as I know, it is not even properly audited,

I still think that the English Ford management would have done better in1962 – 63 if it hadn't been hypnotized by money like a frightened rabbit. I thought it was silly not to challenge Al Baume's study in order to get a better deal. My productivity comparisons in Germany and Britain were as far as possible based on the real economy, by trying as best I could, to get to purchasing power parity costings. I believe this could have been explained to Henry Ford himself. He seemed to me to be a very intelligent man. I do believe he would have listened and would have understood the economic point. He must have inherited the first Henry Ford's sound grasp of practical economics.

But even in Dagenham Central Finance Staff no one really believed he would listen any more. One departmental head I talked to, Brian Tolmie, just shrugged his shoulders and said "The Americans are our masters". Some of the directors were taken with my study, notably Stanley Elliott. The decision whether to send it onward was really John Barber's. He simply said it was not "suitable for management" – ie engineers wouldn't understand it. Maybe not. I think though the clever thing would have been to have shown it to Al Baume - I think he would have moderated his views, because I was able to fault his analysis. He would not have been able to risk ignoring this, or so it still seems to me. There was a final discussion with Ron East, departmental head, and Mr Riordan, Assistant Controller. Ron East was a good economist who had been sent to university by Ford of England after having worked there as a young recruit. He knew far more about the company than I did, though I dont think he had any experience of this sort of economic study. In any case he thought it unwise to question the Americans.

To clinch the matter, as he wished, he rang a well-known woman economist, and asked her in principle, how reliable was this sort of study. She quite correctly replied that this sort of thing was always debatable. I would not have argued against her – my point was that there was no reason to suppose that Al Baume's study was any more "reliable" than mine. The whole point for me was to show Henry Ford that another opinion was *possible.* Economics is a guide in uncertainty, but *it cannot remove uncertainty.*

I believe if we had passed the study to Al Baume, he would have had to concede as much. I think that had someone at Dearborn then said to Henry Ford that Dagenham had a different view to Baume's he would have pricked up his ears, asked to see the studies or a resume of them and adjudicated. The matter would then have got back to the real point of all this. Was it better for Ford to work with Germans or with the English? Henry was Irish ... Ive no idea what he would have decided. But he could well have reduced the switch of funds to Köln. Brian Tolmie stayed on. Riordan retired. I dont know what happened to Ron East. Derek Whittaker went to British Leyland; a great many good mangers went elsewhere.

6.1 The Supply of Money.

Every year there are increases in industrial capacity. This means more goods can be produced. This means we need more money in circulation. But there is no *mechanism* to make that happen automatically. No one in the banking system knows how much will be produced each year! So, *ex post*, they have to accord *credit* when growth takes place. This enables them to have a "cut" on the increased national "net product" by charging interest. If the money system worked automatically as ideally it should, that would not happen. Businesses obviously know this is how things are. Would they need credit to expand if they were *self-financed?* Self-financing does *not* please un-engaged shareholders! If you buy a share because you want a money return **this** year, you are not going to like it if the company tells you "sorry, nothing this year, as we have to finance an expansion in capacity". A rich man with plenty of money might take a longer view. Would the economy function better if rich people became entrepreneurs and used their money to start up new companies, instead of lending it out at interest? Well, by and large, they don't – that is why we have a massive expansion of the financial sector. It is perhaps arguable that maybe we don't really need a financial sector at all. Once you understand this inherent problem, you will understand better what is going on in the world of high finance.

Although this is often overlooked, the vast majority of money transactions are quite small, since most of them will be at retail level; most of them are consumer purchases of necessities. In most areas of the world these necessities tend to be *locally* produced. *At this level, the world is not one economy at all.* In many states, the economy largely consists of small transactions in local products. The currency value has settled to a value which suits these transactions.

I have already cited a practical example from my army service in Egypt in 1951 – 52. Local prices for Egyptian workers were far, far lower than prices in Britain. That was why the then Egyptian pound had to be divided into **thousandths**, so that there could be coins small enough to be useable in Egyptian villages. Do you see now how exchange rates can **distort** reality. To reflect reality better they would need to be adjusted to *purchasing power parity*. That isn't straight forward either. The Egyptian lived on chapattis, (like you get in some Indian restaurants) and little lumps of meat mixed with peppers and garlic. How would you establish purchasing power parity with a London workers fish and chips (or a century ago "boiled beef and carrots".)

Much of the real economy isn't easily commensurable in money. Economists have to live in a world of *approximations, half truths* and sheer *guesswork.* When someone tells you that workers, in this or that far off country, are paid less than in Europe, ask your informant this question "And aren't entrepreneurs and landlords and government tax collectors also paid less too?" Because if they are, that must mean that the exchange rate on international currency markets has *diverged* from purchasing power parity.

Now that you understand this, you will see why a world money would have to be established at the best guess economists could make of all the purchasing power parities of all the world's currencies. And when that had been done, it might still be found they hadn't got it quite right – adjustments would be difficult later! The Euro has probably had all these problems , but as far as I know , no one has studied the consequential effects of merging the previous European currencies into one at international exchange rates, instead of purchasing power parities. You see, international exchange rates are determined by only those goods which cross international frontiers, and are unaffected by all the goods that *don't!* Hence the divergence.

I have been getting anecdotal reports from friends that although Ireland and France are both "in" the Euro, prices in Ireland, after a decade, still remain higher than in France. Might this have been avoided if the punt had been converted into Euros at purchasing power parity. I don't know myself – a study would have to be done. As Ireland was finding it a great strain to comply with Brussels' directives, and had asked for some moderation of them, I thought it might be a good idea if I pointed out that such a study might be helpful. It might get the Eurocrats to budge from their entrenched position – positions developed, I would point out, on the mistaken assumption that money is *primary*. The Taoiseach, Enda Kenny, kindly passed my letter to the Finance Minister,

Michael Noonan. He replied that the causes of the "banking crisis" in Ireland had been studied by various economists. So I wrote back asking him to ask these economists whether they had taken purchasing power parities into account. As I write, I am awaiting his reply. The point for you dear reader, is that you can now begin to see the importance of purchasing power parity. A wrong decision a decade ago could still be affecting Ireland today.

Let us assume a *world money* could be established, taking good account of the foregoing issues. Any residual problem would in the end be eased, if there was a substantial burst of worldwide economic growth – a worldwide Wirtschaftswunder.

Now deflation is like anorexia and inflation like bulimia. Good monetary government is obliged to get the balance exactly right. Not to be optimistic, nor to be pessimistic, but just to be *objective* and as *exact* as possible. Herein lies a problem. Borrowers are optimists. They probably have to be. Lenders are pessimists: they certainly are wise, so to be. Banks are lenders. (They have to borrow to lend, but have no problem since everyone likes to have their money in a safe place. High street banks in fact have to fight quite hard to find enough people to lend to! High street banks however, are regulated by their central bank. If the central bank gets the total money supply right, there should be no great problem. (Maybe some banks are over-branched, but they can correct that themselves.)

But can the central bank get the money supply right? Not always, or so it would seem. The European Central Bank went on **raising interest rates,** and so restricting the money supply, right into the eye of the financial storm which started in 2008, and has not yet (2012) abated. Had they not done this, the said storm might never have crossed the Atlantic from the U.S! I don't know for sure – but that does seem at least possible. *Excessive caution does damage to the economy.* It increases unemployment and the mere fact that we have *any* unemployment at all is probably a sign of excessive caution. Bankers run not only the central banks, but also the International Monetary Fund and the World Bank. In the 1970s I suspect the I.M.F. must have been too over-cautious vis-à-vis Britain – which had full employment until then, but has had unemployment ever since. (In the 70s I was *astonished,* walking in a side street off the Strand to see a man foraging in a dustbin. **I had never in all my life seen that before!)**

here are those who still argue that if we don't have unemployment we will have inflation. But throughout the thirty years after the victory in Europe we had moderate inflation and full employment. The one bad inflation only occurred when decimalization was badly handled, as I believe. Instead of switching to a new currency unit of one hundred old pence – the rational way to decimalize – the ill-advised decision was taken to convert a pound of 240 old pence to one of 100 new ones. As already mentioned most daily transactions are very *small* ones. So daily necessities priced in old pence and shillings had to be converted into new pence. Often, there was no *exact* conversion possible, so *businesses* ***rounded their prices up.*** With this rounding up affecting a huge number of daily small transactions, there was an immediate widespread price inflation. Such things are easy to start but much harder to stop. Probably much of the high inflation since then was caused by this.

Let me give an example;

TYPICAL PRICE OF MODEL LOCOMOTIVE

1967	1986	1994	2012
£7	£32	£56	£125

Source; various Model Railway journals

I wonder how much of that ongoing inflation has resulted from the initial "kick" given by the wrong decimalization decision. It would need a specially detailed study to find out, but I suspect we may still be living with that mistake and its effects. Of course, it could also be argued that oligopoly has played its part. There is one large manufacturer of model engines in Britain, also owning brands which were previously Continental. An old-established German company went broke a couple of years ago. Others soldier on. *But in 1967 there were far more such producers.*

Yet my closing comment on this example would be that there would be less oligopoly and less continuance of old inflationary "kick" had there not been what I would judge to be persistent *excessive caution* by both U.S. and European monetary authorities. I am not arguing a case for any major adjustment, the balance between excessive and objective monetarism is really quite fine. A small but continuous percentage increase in the money supply would probably be all that is needed to maintain full employment (and thereby increase government revenue from taxes.) That's how important it is to manage money carefully.

In one case *restricting* the supply of money seems, oddly enough, to have provoked growth! This was in Western Germany in 1948. The occupying western powers rightly or wrongly, took it into their heads to "reform" the currency in their zones. Possibly they expected the Russians to follow suit. The Soviets were not entirely against currency reform; Soviet occupied Hungary had just recently had a quite effective one. But Russian economists presumably judged the situation differently from American ones – *Hence the subsequent partition of Germany!* Anyway the Wirtschaftswunder followed. To this day people in Germany believe that this is somehow **because** of the currency reform. But France, Italy and the Benelux all enjoyed much the same rate of growth at that time without restricting their own supply! In the case of both France and Italy, there were in fact repeated *devaluations!* The real cause of the growth in all the six countries must have been in the real economy and not in the money reflection at all.

6.2 Banks, Cheques and Credit Cards

It will no doubt astonish you, dear reader, to learn that I am rather dubious about electronic money! Probably you will think that I am just old fashioned, at the age of 83 as I put the finishing touches to the book. There may be some truth in that perhaps, but I would still urge you to reflect on what I say, because there are fundamental theoretical points involved.

Money has to be *managed. This is not exactly easy!* The government and the central bank have to balance the interests of **all** sectors of the economy. Too much attention, too many favours to this or that sector, can in fact hamper the other sectors – and maybe thereby slow the economy down. That is the danger which all the time must be guarded against. This is particularly tricky in any period of crisis.

All crises can only originate in the real economy. That at least is what I happen to believe. (Other economists may disagree.) I shall deal with that issue more fully in chapter 8. But first let us see how one particular sector of the economy, banking, functions. It may be important at times to balance the interests of the banks against the interests of other sectors of the economy. Which is why I am dubious about electronic money, which speeds up the rate at which money changes hands? Does the rest of the economy really *need* this rate to be accelerated? Myself, I think not.

Some years ago, I had to check on the procedures involved if I were to accept a payment in South African rands. In part of the correspondence, I managed to elicit a letter from the E.U. in Brussels. Apparently the cheque was regarded there as somehow being "inefficient" means of payment! Or so the writer of the letter said.

What an **extraordinary** thing to say! All payments result from some sort of *compromise!* What is efficient for the creditor may not be at all efficient for the debtor! There may be in any case no particular urgency involved: for example, if one is paying an advance subscription for a magazine. But even when there is a reasonable need for the payment to be received quickly, in practice there are all sorts of delays. In the book trade, bookshops demand 60 days credit as of right, and then expect to be slowish in paying for books they have probably already sold. They would obviously prefer to pay, when they finally do, by cheque, Thus adding a still further three days on to the credit accorded, while the cheque is cleared. ("Cross-border cheques in the E.U. take even longer as there is *still* no Euro bank clearing system after 10 years, as I write,)

The longer the better say the payers! Some payers who cost their time might even add that they can sign a cheque and put it in an envelope and post it, more quickly than sending an electronic transfer, which can involve writing out and verifying all the unbelievably long numbers in use. Moreover the time taken to clear a cheque is important also for the banks. The possibly extremist measure of prohibiting credit cards is unlikely to be taken, but if it were, bank liquidity would be *eased*, globally and tremendously! This is because in the massive total of daily transactions, *small* payments make up a very large portion – as I've already pointed out. This simple and obvious fact is, however, often ignored by governments! A notable example was provided when the UK decimalized its currency many years ago. Decimalization meant *rounding up* all small prices from prices in old pennies (240 to the £) to prices in new pennies (100 to the £). The result was a *massive globalized inflationary pressure* throughout both the UK and Ireland (At the time Ireland still used the British currency).

What to do? I myself suggest the following:-

a) the cheque should be *retained* and indeed *encouraged* so that payers can use it whenever they prefer to

b) banks should not be allowed to charge any commission on crediting accounts with cheques

c) this should apply even when the cheque is in another currency: banks should only be able to charge the difference between buying and selling exchange rates.

Of course this would cost the banks more! But *banks would also have some extra funds which could be lent at call or short notice.* And the economy as a whole would benefit as the "velocity of money" would be slowed down, thus *moderating* inflationary pressures. The comment from the Brussels official is, to say the least, *puzzling*! Whoever drafted it, evidently knew little about monetary economics. A cheque is merely a special form of a bill of exchange. Bills of exchange have existed since the dawn of history, and will continue to exist as long as we have money. All a bill of exchange is, is a means of *requesting* credit.

When I worked at the Bank of China in 1952 – 60, I had a slim book, issued by one of the London discount houses, explaining bills of exchange. I cannot remember its title. If you have a sufficiently good search engine, you might be able to discover it, because I do recall that its extremely able author quoted **Kipling** – something to the effect that there were "960 ways of constructing tribal lays, and every single one of them is right". There were as many ways of composing bills of exchange.

Apparently some banks believe that they can "abolish" the cheque. I hope my bank, currently AIB, will have more *sense!* It can't ever hope to stop me writing out a letter which says something like this

"Dear Supplier,

this letter is an *instruction* to my bank in Leopards town to pay its bearer the sum of [say] twenty three euros and 65 cents.

Yours sincerely

[Signature]"

If the bank refused to obey my instruction, I'd close the account and take my money elsewhere! (I do however accept that the bank could reasonably stipulate terms for a cheque format **if** the account was in *overdraft* – but not if it was in credit.)

Don't think, dear reader, that I am inventing this, out of my own head. Get your search engine to work again! Scan the local paper in Maidstone in the mid-60s! The National Westminster branch there, perhaps to mark the merger of the Westminster and National Provincial banks, did a publicity stunt in Maidstone High Street. *It had a cheque written on an egg.* (I knew someone at this branch, because he and I both sat on the committee of the Maidstone Productivity Council. I was sufficiently impressed by the stunt to have a word with him and so transfer my own account there, to his branch!) The stunt was legally perfectly sound. You could, if you so wished, write a cheque on an egg ...

To come back to this ill-informed official in Brussels, *if a debtor wishes to ask for credit from a supplier, why shouldn't he?* And even if the supplier tells the customer that he'll send the goods when he's cashed the cheque, credit still comes into it! He may even have to make the goods while the cheque is in transit, or at lest he must earmark them for the customer – who still has the benefit that his account won't be debited until the cheque arrives! With electronic money, he looses that benefit. Frankly, that official was a bit silly to say such a thing! *All exchange involves compromise!*

So that's why I am against electronic money. Moreover, I cannot bring myself to believe that in the ultimate analysis it can ever be really *safe*. A hand written cheque is surely much safer? Because its harder to forge. All the advocates of electronic money can say to reassure me is that there are *codes* which "cannot" be cracked, to make cars safe. To which I reply that the Wehrmacht thought it had uncrackable codes in 1939 – 45. The Wehrmacht was *wrong!* The post war mainframe computers were developed as a by-product of the computer which was used by the allies to crack the German codes!) It seems to me that anyone with a good enough computer will sooner or later crack *any* code! If fraudulent hackers succeed, they could manufacture cards mimicking **your** credit card ...I may be totally wrong.
But the theoretical point is that to function properly, money does need to be safe, for sure ...

When the Euro was being introduced, everyone expected to cash cheques freely over the whole Eurozone. I certainly did. At the time I received cheques in sterling and paid them in to one of two accounts, one with Banque Scalbert-Dupont in France, one with the AIB in Ireland.

The announcement of the introduction of the Euro stated, among other things, that one could ask one's bank to change one's account into Euros *immediately*. So I requested both banks to do this. *Neither bank ever replied!* They both just ignored my letter! I still find that puzzling. Having a single currency should greatly increase the total volume of banking transactions in Europe. The banks would thereby have more funds in their coffers, and more business for which they could charge normal commissions. They'd ***benefit!*** Well, that's what I thought! (Is my trouble that being an economist, and so using my acquaintanceship with economic principles in making all sorts of decisions, I expect other people to do the same?)

It still puzzles me why from the word go, banks were so obstructively un-enthusiastic about the Euro. Its only a currency. Having one currency across the whole Eurozone makes life a lot easier for each countries exporters and importers, and so inter-zone trade ought to have risen dramatically.

It didn't.

Why ever not? I'm sure I don't know. Someone should do a lot of detailed studies to find out.. Myself, I suspect the bank's total lack of *vision* is at least a significant contributory cause. The whole point of having the European Union was to make the economy grow like crazy. There should have been a new *Wirtschaftswunder.* Only this time for *all* of Europe, from the Shetlands to Spain, from Achill Island to Athens. Were we wrong to bother with the European project? Surely, we shouldn't have been?

As I write, European banks **charge commission** on what they choose to call "cross-border" cheques. This is totally ridiculous. Not only have borders been in effect *abolished within Europe;* charging any commission at all is **senseless**!

When I pay in any cheque to my bank, I am lending them my money, at any point in time that my account is in credit. If my account is in credit, the bank apparently thinks it's a good idea to charge me for lending them money. Are they completely crazy? *The total of all cheques deposited with the banking system can immediately be lent out at call or short notice on the money market.* I mentioned Bert Dennet at Fords having great fun, moving Fords £60 million around from one short term security to another. Someone somewhere in every bank HQ can have that fun. It's quite *exhilarating*! It also earns interest.

What I wonder is the bank's problem? French banks charge **penal** commissions on such cheques! In the pre-electronic days, a large part of any banks liquid assets was lent at call and short notice. When I was at the Bank of China, I worked for a while in the banking hall and every morning, I think it would have been around 10.30 to 11.00, an imposing tall gentleman *wearing a top hat* would stroll in, exchange a few brief words with our chief cashier and walk out again. He was a representative of one of the discount houses, and he would take any of the previous day's surplus cash and pay interest on it on very short terms.

The whole structure of British banking was then very hierarchical. There were 5 major banks, who lent to these discount houses in this way. Whenever the whole system was "short", the Bank of England would lend to fill the gap, *at Bank Rate.* By changing bank Rate up or down, the Bank of England could restrict or relax the total credit available in the economy. This system was thoroughly investigated by the Radcliffe Committee Report in the later 50s. (At the Bank of China, this report was thought sufficiently important for the entire Economics Department to spend about a fortnight, I think it was, working through it) This system worked smoothly and well, from a technical point of view. There were then no "shadow" banks, and established banks simply did not indulge in *risky* investments! A current popular joke then was "You can borrow as much on overdraft as you like so long as you can prove you don't need it". The whole prevailing money culture was *cautious.* People saved rather than borrowed. House mortgages were only handled by specialized companies and not by banks at all. I don't think any bank clerks were then judged by their superiors by how much money they had lent out last week! How different from the contemporary scene as I write.

Then only the middle class had bank accounts. Now everyone has one. The payments were made largely by cheque. Now we have electronic money. Then moreover most, people did not borrow from their bank. The bank was mainly used to keep your money safe. Now banks seem upset if you don't borrow from them up to the hilt. Probably it is the credit card which has brought all this about. As I say, they reduce bank liquidity. Then there was money lying around *inert.* This continuing volume was in effect the principal source of funds lent at call and short notice. Now we have a frantic drive all the time to find more and more borrowers. The problem is that whereas the discount houses, backed up by the Bank of England were extremely safe, "other borrowers " are not! Hence we have banking crises! Detailed studies need to be done. The point is that there is now an *inherent instability* in the banking system. In the old days middle class people thought it silly to buy something this month when you could easily pay for it next month *without borrowing.* Then only the middle class had bank accounts. (The working class borrowed weekly from people who were little better than loan sharks). Now both middle and working classes habitually borrow just a month ahead with credit cards. For the working classes this is an improvement, of course. For the middle classes they started on credit cards a few years ago because they were a status symbol ... but they aren't anymore.

Maybe we should go back to a more savings oriented culture? Might it help economic growth if we did? And aren't we all really being a trifle manic?

Businesses only need credit ridden customers for one simple reason: the "supply" of money doesn't comfortably match the actual capacity of manufacturing industry. Bankers will object strongly to this remark. They will argue that to relax the "supply" of money would generate inflation. Of course they think of the quantity of money as being a "supply". As we have seen, that isn't quite right. On the contrary, if the "supply" isn't "comfortable", wouldn't the logical thing be to ease it? The problem is *oligopoly.* We don't have enough competition. Even slightly less imperfect competition would make easier money safe.

I once received a letter from a bank describing a current account as a "product". This is nonsense. It isn't a product: banks don't produce anything. A bank account is a *loan.* I lend my money to the bank. I lend it "at call". Any time I want it, I can have it back. I could put my money in a box in the strong room. But I'd have to pay for that. It costs money to build, maintain and service a strong room. However, my primary motive is to keep my money safe so that it can act as a "store of value" for me. Whether it really acts as a store of value however depends on whether there is much inflation. It was a waste of time putting money in a bank during the German run-away inflation!

When banking started, the only money was coin. Then paper money arrived. Nowadays much of the money paid into one bank account comes by means of a transfer from another bank account.

Do you notice anything, dear reader?

The receiving bank only has the paying bank's word for it that they have the money in their vaults to "back" the transfer. No notes need necessarily move from one bank to the other. What happens in fact is that all the entries in both directions are totted up each day, not only for these two banks but for all the banks in what is called a clearing system. At the end of each day, *net* transfers are made from one bank to another as appropriate. Still little "actual" money moves anywhere.

The main movement of actual money , coin or notes, is into or out of the banking system as a whole from or to "holders" who are not banks e.g.;

a) Shopkeepers bank their day's takings

b) You need to have some cash in your pocket; you go to a "hole-in-the-wall" cash machine and draw some notes out. (You get coins mostly in change when you buy something.)

Do you see what is happening? Money is largely just a book-keeping entry. It has been like this for well over a century. To be quite brutal, the whole set-up is a house of cards.

6.3 The Velocity of Money.

Any given quantity of money, however carefully controlled, can have inflationary effects if the rate at which it changes hands speeds up. (This rate is called the velocity of money)

Electronic money automatically speeds up the velocity of money, and to that extent is in itself inflationary. The very existence of electronic money moreover means that if, for whatever reason, there were to be a lack of confidence in the currency, the velocity could shoot up suddenly and rapidly. Control of the **quantity** would become ineffective if that happened; the quantity is in effect multiplied by the velocity. A feature of the German run-away inflation in the 1920s was the speed at which workers spent their wages. This was self-accelerating because prices could rise sharply the day after payday. Had there been electronic money in those days, the inflation would have been even worse.

In any large currency zone such as the Eurozone, this is a constant risk. Moreover the problem could be worse in Europe than it could ever be in large unitary states like the U.S., China, India, Brazil or Russia. Confidence in a large unitary state is likely to be evenly spread over the whole country; but Europe consists of a large number of independent sovereign states, who do not necessarily trust each other all that much. Old enmities and dislikes mean a low level of trust between some "pairs" of countries. There is little trust between Greeks and Turks, for both historical and recent reasons; if Turkey were to join Europe, that situation would take years to ameliorate. (I have to wonder if it is not a good thing for the stability of the world currency markets that Britain has *not* joined the Euro,)

The banking crises in Greece, Spain, Portugal and Ireland have further diminished trust. If there were to be any factor disturbing confidence, such as a war in the Middle East, the Euro could face a sudden inflationary crisis caused by a sudden upsurge in the velocity of money. I believe the "cross border" use of electronic money should be restricted and other restrictions might quite conceivably be imposed.. Moreover they would need to be established discreetly, via *strictly confidential* instructions from the European Central Bank to the various banks in the various states. The reason for confidentiality is that any public announcement of such measures could easily provoke a run on the Euro.

6.4 Origins of Money.

Money started by being just another commodity. But this commodity started being held on to, for its own sake, as well as its utility. It had qualities which made it handy both to keep by for future exchanges and as more permanent "store of value", if it was sufficiently durable. Of course, as we have seen, value being subjective is not so easy to "store" ... Cattle were so used , and in parts of Africa continued to be until recent times. An interesting study was made in the late 40s of the way in which cigarettes became an effective currency in prisoner of war camps. (Published in the learned journal *Economica*)

But because of their exceptional durability, gold and silver came to be the main commodities used, and were soon "fixed" for the purpose by the invention of coinage. Paper money followed in time; at first in England, it was a promise to pay in gold coin if required. However many governments, short of cash, were not above printing more paper money than was really justified. As long as only a few people sought to convert the paper into gold, this didn't seem to matter very much. But if there was a lack of confidence, the invalidity of any excessive issue of paper money would soon be shown up. If you could no longer get gold for it, you bought anything you could lay your hands on, as a "store of value", you hoped. Prices rocketed, so seemingly your hope justified itself, and would continue to do so as long as what you had bought did not deteriorate, and so long as its price did not fall.

In the German run-away inflation, the whole situation got completely out of hand. A French bank study I had to translate in the mid 50s claimed there was some danger of this sort of thing happening in France.

But it was headed off when devaluation proved sufficient to stabilize the situation. Curiously enough, the Bank of England, not withstanding the German example, stopped paying out gold against notes but managed to avoid losing confidence, even though the old gold coins disappeared.

Most countries now have only paper money in circulation, but backed by gold "reserves" held by the Central Bank, and used to pay off net debits to other currencies. So we still, in the last analysis, use gold.

6.5 Why have money?

The reason we need money is to make exchanges. In a modern economy there are more exchanges each day than there are stars in the sky. This is because we have an extremely complicated "division of labour" – or you could call it a system of reciprocity. To put it, so to speak, by looking through the wrong end of the telescope, if each and every individual could produce all that he needed, we would not need economic reciprocity at all.

Probably for the first million or so years that the species *Homo sapiens* has been on the planet, such reciprocity as was needed could be contained in small tribal groups. But now the whole planet is really one economy, though as yet the fullest possible division of labour has not been achieved. (I expect it will be eventually.) This is what makes reciprocity such an extraordinarily powerful force, so powerful that some have seen it as evil; read for example the diatribe against money in Shakespeare's *Timon of Athens*. Christ's teaching was more restrained: while he instructed us that we could not *serve* both God and Mammon, he made the important qualification that one must render unto Caesar, that which is Caesar's. Sound economic theory! We can only have money if we have state power to back it, and we need it for human society to function, although some have dreamt that it will one day be possible to dispense with it, notably William Morris in his book News *from Nowhere.*

Am I straying outside the realm of economics proper? Not at all. Economics cannot be understood unless we first grasp that money is an extremely powerful cultural force. This is true whatever one's ethos. It is true for Buddhists and for atheists, for Moslems and Hindus, for Teague and Prod.

Ask yourself, could we run such an extraordinarily complicated world economy as we now have without money? As an exercise try and imagine a moneyless society, and search for answers to the following questions:-

- How would we each find work?
- How could anyone calculate, let alone plan, how much of each highly specialized kind of work needed to be done each day, across the surface of the globe?
- How much of each myriad different commodity would need to be produced each day?

The money system signals answers to these questions in all the multitudinous markets of the economy. It does this, so to speak, pragmatically. Maybe it does not always provide sufficiently accurate answers. Do ponder these questions, dear reader ...

I have twice lived in, so to speak, embryo moneyless societies. For two years I was a conscript in the British Army, rising, I am still a little proud to say, to the dizzy rank of Sergeant (acting) R.A.O.C. This was some years after the war. What I witnessed was a mere aftermath of a much larger embryo, established to fight and as it turned out, win the Second World War.

One could not run large military "machines" without establishing a moneyless situation. One could not win battles if commanding officers had to ring up distant factories and order more bullets, and open a letter of credit with some handy bank to pay for these bullets as they were shipped to (say) Egypt. The war would be lost long before the bullets had got through the Bay of Biscay.

The Eighth Army, holding Rommel at El Alamein had recently lost a lot of supplies, when the Germans overran an ordnance depot; I think it would have been at or near Tobruk in Libya. Fortunately Rommel was also short of supplies, being a long way from home. As Britain had virtual command of the sea, Montgomery's supplies were being replenished and augmented by enormous quantities, in ship loads, delivered to Port Said and then taken by train to a very large port at Tel el Kebir., reasonably safely behind the front line, on the opposite side of the Delta to El Alamein. As I say, I served there in 1951 – 52. It really was big. It was thirty miles round the perimeter. It had to be divided into four "sub-depots" to make such an enormous quantity of stores manageable, each sub-depot being responsible for a particular class of supplies. For example, number 4 sub-depot was responsible for tents, tents of every imaginable size and arrangement. And all these supplies were doled out to the front line in huge quantities if necessary, without money changing hands. It was "to each according to his needs" to quote Lenin's famous idealistic future. And because everyone wanted to win the war, the Army in return got "from each according to his abilities". To complete the way in which the Utopian dream would one day, it was hoped, actually function. But it wasn't Utopia. It was the Western Desert in 1943. It did *work*. Montgomery drove Rommel all the way back from El Alamein, through Libya and well in to Tunisia.

But at what **cost!**

Huge mountains of stores remained unused in the depot at Tel el Kebir. They were still there when I did my military service as Depot Statistician in 1952-53. An amazing return I had to render every month was to report the total **volume** of stores, measured by their *cubic size!!* It no longer mattered very much what the stores really were. They were government property, so some sort of account had to be kept of them. To a small extent they were still being used by the British Army which still occupied the Canal Zone. That occupation ended a couple of years later. I've no idea what happened to the stores. The point is that was what a moneyless society would be like. Would it often produce so much that some of it would be wasted?

Marx, in his early youth, opined that the use of money was against human nature. Shaw – quite as left-wing as Marx – once told someone, "If a thing is for the good of humanity, it will show a profit". And Marx himself praised the ability of capitalism to increase industrial capacity. What do you think, dear reader?

As a student, I spent my first summer vacation working in another embryo moneyless society. The Yugoslav government had persuaded its own young people to have a "holiday" working on the "Autoput Bratsltvo-Jedinstvo" (The Brotherhood-Unity Motorway) between Zagreb, the catholic capital of Croatia, and Belgrade the orthodox capital of Serbia. (Although Yugoslavia was technically "communist", it was in reality an attempt by modernizing free-thinkers to unite Serbs and Croats into one country. With some minor differences in dialect, they had a common language – but were ravaged by grotesquely various confessional conflicts, some of which were chronicled by Brigadier Fitzroy MacLean in his work "Eastern Approaches". Part of the idea of this holiday work scheme was to bring Serbs and Croats together in a common project – hence the slogan Bratstvo-Jedinstvo. A slogan shouted out repeatedly at the tops of their voices. If I had a pound for every time I heard those 2 words in four weeks, I would be a wealthy man. Do you see the point, dear reader? This was a little chunk of *economic* policy, concocted with both political and economic ends:-

a) unite the fissiparous country

b) build an important motorway.

Note that b) worked but a) did not. Not untypical of government policies.

How we all came to go was because the Yugoslav government, needing as many unskilled workers as possible, so as to build the motorway as quickly as possible, invited young people from other countries. We met fellow students from Denmark and from Trieste (then under Allied military occupation, as it was disputed between Yugoslavia and Italy). Once inside the frontier, we didn't have to pay anything.

We got free train journeys to the camp site, with free food, including a nice restaurant meal in Ljubljana en route, and more food on the train at Zagreb. While there we were fed and allocated bunks in dormitories. For us, of course, it was fun. We could sun ourselves and pursue our student love affairs in relaxed conditions. And it was moneyless. For the Yugoslav youth, it thrived, apparently, on the tremendous "spirit" still to be found in Continental countries in 1948. It was still fresh in people's minds that they were delivered from that terrible war, which for the Yugoslavs was especially joyful as they saw themselves as having liberated their country themselves, with a little bit of help form their British and Russian friends.

After 4 weeks we got a free four-day holiday on the Dalmatian coast, and were taken by train to the Italian frontier at Udine. Did any of us speculate whether *all* of society could be run in this way? Probably not! And if in retrospect, I ask myself the question, I have to come to the conclusion that it worked for a short while and in limited circumstances only because of this overflow of the Victory-in-Europe spirit. Dear reader, by all means pursue your own reflections.

Communism was intended to become a moneyless society. That was why Lenin changed the name of the Russian Social Democratic Party to "Communist" Party (or so he said). Stalin continued to declare that this was his aim too. That was why the kolkhoz was pushed so hard. It was there to prepare the way towards a moneyless agriculture. (Others have commented the similarity with the former Israeli kibbutz.) But how was one to get there? How was a moneyless society to be achieved? By "building Soviet man" Stalin would reply. "Social engineering" was gradually to create people with responses like the imagined men and women in Morris's *News from Nowhere.* After Stalin's death, all this was quietly forgotten. It does rather seem, does it not, as if we are stuck with money, short of the second coming and the establishment of Christ's Eternal Kingdom...

And if we are stuck with money, are we not perhaps stuck with Capitalism, and with the Economics Quincunx.

6. 6 The Value of Money.

I think the reader can take it as a fact that there is a continual "secular" tendency for the purchasing power of *metal- based* money to diminish.

Would this trend not continue even if my notion of a single world currency with one world central bank could be achieved, so that the world supply of money could be continually adjusted to meet the world increase in industrial capacity? It seems just possible to me that if this was properly and skilfully done, prices might even tend to fall. But I don't know. The only way to find out would be to try it and see. I beg leave to doubt if we ever will!

But prices are about scarcity. If there were fewer and fewer scarcities, prices should surely decline. May be if we could extrapolate far enough into the future we would come towards a world in which prices had little meaning.

Recapitulation so far.

Meanwhile, economic problems manifest as apparently monetary problems. Yet problems in the real economy are not much helped by tinkering with money. Economics is about living. That is why value is subjective because valuations can only be made by living human beings.

That prices seem to be somehow "objective", and are said to be "fixed" by market forces is illusory. "Market forces" are nothing but the summing up of the interactions of what every living member of the species wants. Different people want different things, and so compromises have to be reached, daily, hourly, minute by minute. If we were to rethink what we want out of life, market forces and the whole world economy would thereby be *changed.* Money is secondary to all that.

6. 7 The German Inflation of the 1920s.

I think that this can be seen particularly clearly in this runaway inflation. It was produced by very unusual "wants". The French having won the war blamed the Germans for starting it. (This was rather unfair. Actually it was the Austrians who started it by reacting to the killing of an Archduke at Sarajevo, by a Serb who felt the Austrians should never have occupied Bosnia-Herzegovina.)

The French demanded that damages done to French property during the German incursion into Northern France should be repaired. (The word "reparation" is the French word for "repair".)

So the French confiscated a large part of the German locomotive stock. At that time, the railway was virtually the only means of bulk land transport, apart from barges. The German government had to replace the confiscated locomotives. The old railways of the various states, large and small, were amalgamated into the Reichsbahn. This at least meant that locomotives could be standardized into a small number of types, whereas previously, each railway, large or small, had its own types, in too many varieties. The German locomotive manufacturers thus achieved significant increase in productivity, because there were great economies of scale in this standardization. Thus it was that while outside their factories, workers were having to take home pay in pram loads of worthless notes, and spend them as quickly as possible before prices rose still further, the real economy of the locomotive manufacturing industry *forged steadily on.* The currency failed because the German government had little alternative but to print these worthless notes. Those with only money savings lost the lot. **Money ceased altogether to be a source of value.** But even in a runaway inflation, the real economy still plodded on. Money is secondary.

Early on in the history of money, it came to be used as a "store" of value. But it has never been a good one, though seldom quite so bad as in 1920s Germany. You see, as world industrial capacity increases, either the supply of money must increase *pro rata* or there will probably be inflation. We do not have a choice, really. Short of my idea of a world central bank regulating money supply realistically, there will always be some inflation. Trying to prevent that by allowing unemployment to rise doesn't provide any solution at all – it simply doesn't work.

You would think the well-informed rich would have learnt that lesson by now. The best thing they can do with their wealth is to buy up large companies, and turn them into private family companies. (They would have to run them well!) But their money would be safer than in loans. You'd think the Greek crisis would have taught them that, wouldn't you?

Unfortunately, economists do not, as I write, seem to think it is necessary to tell the rich this. I find that rather sad. The rich can use economic advice as much as the rest of us – and it would be to everyone's advantage if they did. Rich and poor might then make more advantageous compromises. Why aren't economists speaking out? I myself wonder whether the universities are not making something of a mistake in focusing on "applied" economics as they seem to do.

For my money, I think it is philosophically *debateable* whether we can divide economics into pure and applied, as is done with mathematics and physics. Surely only the real economy can be the subject matter of economics. "Applied" economics turns out to be the study of money *in isolation.* I dont think that is very sensible. It is only with their relationships with other points in the quincunx that monetary events can be understood.

6. 8 How money prices attach to real goods

Goods are primary: money is secondary. If you doubt this, reflect that goods are still useful if not exchanged for money. But money is useless unless there are things to buy with it. It is a cliché, a truism, that prices are determined by what is called "supply" and "demand". Real people supply things; other people demand them.

"Supply" and demand" sound like abstractions, but they aren't really. They are better understood as aspects of the real economy, which consists of *people*.

If economic commentators total these aspects, it is well to remember that each individual my have different needs and wants, and that even when a number of imdividuals have similar demands to make, they may put different valuationms on the same items. While there are generalized needs such as food, clothing, heating, water, etc, market supply and market demand are about a very wide range indeed of specific, separate and variegated items which fall under these very broad categories.

When I was at LSE, teaching stress was on a set of conditions called "perfect competition". The essential *sine qua non* of this concept is a large number of suppliers of pretty well equal size, and a large number of people purchasing from them. Secondary conditions included awareness of what all suppliers were asking. In 1955 I was on a camping holiday in a remote part of County Kerry and wanted to buy potatoes. The woman in the shop asked *me* what were people charging for potatoes! She did not have awareness of other people's prices – unless of course this was a sales ploy of some kind on her part. In a "perfect market", neither lack of awareness or sales ploys could occur. "Perfect" is a *theoretical ideal; we* seldom have it in real life. This doesn't mean the concept is useless. We can construct chains of reasoning to tell us that this and that will happen **if** we have perfect competition.

If we don't have the results which would be obtained from perfect competition, that is very probably because the competition is more or less *imperfect*! If there is imperfect competition, that should be a spur to entrepreneurs to set up new supply companies to get nearer the "perfect" ideal. If they do so, they may be able to undercut the older suppliers, who could have been taking advantage of the imperfections to charge higher prices.

Everyone knows the game "Monopoly". In it, only a few players contest, and very quickly, one or two of them will have more property than the others. But I suppose it is seldom, if ever, that one player owns everything. The better term for this situation would be *oligopoly.* Oligopoly is quite common in highly developed economies; as I write, oligopoly in the West is being challenged by newer economies emerging very rapidly, particularly in Asia. Before long we may have world trade getting a little bit nearer to perfect competition. But whether competition is perfect or not, any and every price is still a compromise between different valuations.

"Value" is not only subjective; it is also partly, if not wholly, qualitative. This proposition needs reflection to understand it fully, and that may take me beyond the scope of this book. Suffice it to say that the difference between one individual's and another's valuations of the same commodity are quite likely to be for *qualitative* reasons.

This affects the theory of competition, which as presented to me 65 years ago (as I write) seemed to assume that a commodity was a commodity and that was that. There are philosophical difficulties about this. If I value a commodity for one quality and someone else values it for a different quality, doesn't that impact on the very concept of competition, if we find, each of us, the same quality in different commodities? Think about that one dear reader. Its only importance in my exposition is to draw your attention to the

ambiguity of the real economy – an ambiguity we tend to overlook if we focus too much on the money reflection, which seems so **un**ambiguous. It is only unambiguous *ex post.* This matters in forecasting. You see, what happens is that we assemble the money/price result of recent compromises between different valuations, and hope that this will guide us in foreseeing future compromises. It may well do so, but only if qualitative factors remain unchanged.

Ford designed the Edsel, a car like other American cars had been since the end of the second world war. But consumer valuations changed abruptly. They didn't like "that sort" of car as much as they did before. Well, that sort of thing does happen of course; but in this instance Ford nearly went bankrupt. They might have still sold the Edsel if they'd slashed the price – but they couldn't afford to.

There is indeed a "law of supply and demand" but it does not have *quantitative* clarity ... Value is not necessarily nor intrinsically quantifiable. If you find this puzzling, that is precisely the point. Human behaviour is puzzling sometimes...

Economic theorists do see all this of course, but point out that money constraints tend to "systematize" behaviour. This certainly used to be true. When incomes were generally rather low, consumers had to rate quantitative value factors far more highly , than qualitative ones – they had little room to manoeuvre. A century later, incomes are much higher at least in developed countries, and the qualitative/quantitative balance is quite probably reversed for many commodities. This affects forecasting. Governments have been relying on forecasting ever since 1945. I wonder how much longer they can continue to do so? Many economists will say I am rather daft to pose that question, but I suspect they are still in the mental trap of supposing that prices are somehow "objective"

Having said all that, the traditional supply and demand analysis is useful when one Is studying any commodity not subject to the vagaries of ultimate consumer valuations.

Such a commodity is tungsten, the chief use of which is in hardening the cutting edge of machine tools. I had to do a little study of the tungsten market when I was working at the Bank of China. In the upward swing of the trade cycle, demand for machine tools would increase disproportionally sharply, and the consequent demand for tungsten shot up. On the supply side, tungsten is mined in a very large number of very small mines, very often operated by people who also work in other ways as well. Some of these small mines are rather high cost. On the upswing, all the small mines would be able to sell their product, even the high cost ones, because prices would rise quite a lot! Demand fell even before the boom started to level off, and collapsed with the downswing. All the high cost mines would cease production altogether, and only resume at the next upswing. The price would then collapse.

I noticed that the upward movement of tungsten prices was a good "lead indicator" of a coming forthcoming boom, but I doubt if the Chinese were very interested in that fact, because, as they saw it then, booms and slumps only mattered to western capitalists. If they were able to make any use at all of my study, it would have been to defer purchases of tungsten until the slump, and then stock enough to last them through the next trade cycle. Of course long term contracts with the high cost producers might have secured somewhat lower prices from them, but that would only be useful if they wanted very large quantities. I don't know what they actually did as a result of my study.

6. 9 Do we need a financial sector?

What an extraordinarily silly questions, any "experts" who read this book will chorus. Do they have a point? Yes and no.

Britain, the first country to have an Industrial Revolution, scarcely had any financial sector at the outset. Moreover what there was had come into some disrepute because of the South Sea Bubble. And it should be remembered that Adam Smith, the founder of modern economics, was rather against the p.l.c. (then called the "joint stock company".) Some large companies were private companies. The glass manufacturer, Pilkington's, was a striking example. Adam Smith's concern was that entrepreneurs should invest their own money. However, the modern stock exchange began to take shape. But how many commentators have paid much attention to the fact that as the financial sector grew, the growth rate of the British economy *slowed down?* A study in the early 1960s by the National institute for Economic and Social Research noted that British growth had ground to a snail's pace before the collection of government economic statistics really started in the second half of the nineteenth century. This means that all the rapid economic growth must have taken place in the late eighteenth and early nineteenth centuries.

We are sometimes told that even in the post-war period, Britain had a "better developed" financial sector than the industrial countries of the Continent. Was that why Britain just plodded along in the 1950s, while the Continental "Six" had a wirtschaftswunder? In 1945 Britain was still richer than the Continent. By the 1970s it was the other way round.

Rapidly growing companies can self-finance. So they need less recourse to the capital market. Some economists have argued that self-finance results in a less efficient apportionment of capital among the various industries. I am not sure about that, though. Is it perhaps true more of companies in a *later* stage of their life cycle? And don't *entrepreneurs* prefer, if they can, to avoid the somewhat irksome caution and "short-term-ness" of unengaged shareholders? My own view for what its worth, is that companies in the first stage of their lifecycle might do better to remain private, if they can. So it is only in the slower, later phases, that a financial sector becomes *necessary* to an industrial economy. I could be wrong, but that's how it seems to me.

6.10 The National Debt

This is really the national capital. In order to run a country, things have to be done which show no apparent return, but which enable the country to function. It has to be defended against attack. It has to be defended against disease. It will need repairs after natural disasters. Its young people will need education. Law courts have to be established for the settlement of disputes. The meetings of the legislature have to have somewhere to assemble, and need staffing to draft bills, print acts and carry out policies. No money will ever come back from these activities in themselves. On the contrary, taxes have to be collected to pay for all the running costs. But the "capital" cost of establishing all this is rather beyond the taxability of the overall economy.

One can of course debate whether all that is done really needs to be done. I myself cannot see why we need Ministries of "Culture", what ever that word is supposed to mean. Of course, my whole analysis of entrepreneurship does indeed suppose an ideological environment which could be labelled "cultural", but I cannot myself fathom how any government body can provide it, nor indeed why government should be expected to do so.

Human society creates its own "culture" in interacting with the material environment in order to survive. This is not to say that the real economy does not need government! And many of the activities of government do have "value": for example, the real economy's benefits from education. These benefits are probably so diffused and so qualitative as to be impossible to quantify, but this does not mean they may not be highly significant. Then there is transport. Even with privatization, the subsidies to railways are still high, and expenditure on maintaining motorways is not inconsiderable. Which all increases taxation. But if it also increases profits, we should set one increase against the other. There might even be a net benefit.

I must not forget the bureaucracy. Is the Civil Service as a whole larger than it need be? Compare the headcount now with what it was (say) 50 years ago, or (say) 100 years ago. Do we really need so many functionaries?

The St Paul of the American Revolution, Tom Paine, made a rather scathing comment on the national debt: "The funding system is not money; neither is it, properly speaking, credit. It in effect, creates upon paper the sum which it appears to borrow, and lays on a tax to keep the imaginary capital alive by the payment of interest and sends the annuity to market, to be sold for money already in circulation. If any credit is given, it is to the disposition of the people to pay the tax, and not to the government, which lays it on. When this disposition expires, what is supposed to be the credit of government expires with it. The instance of France under the former government, shows that it is impossible to compel the payment of taxes by force, when a whole nations is determined to take its stand upon that ground" Tom Paine; **The Rights of Man.** Did he have it right? Maybe what he criticizes in unavoidable?

6. 11 The Money Market, Capital, and the Trade Cycle.

If by putting ones money into a bank one is lending them money, one might ask oneself, why does one have bank charges? Let us think about this. I have already mentioned how English Ford in the early 1960s played the money market with its £64 million "kitty". This money market is varied and efficient. One can lend out money at call, or at any period be it ever so short. With such a money market, interest can be earned even for just one day. Surely all the banks have to do with the money we all lend them is to lend it out again at a return, and so make their living that way? No one with money in a bank draws all of it out. There is always a huge sum of money waiting to be used *one day.* Experience teaches banks how much they can safely lend out for various periods. Broadly speaking this is how it used to be, with only a proportion lent out to private borrowers. Recently, banks have tended to lend out more at higher rates to individuals, on mortgages, credit cards, personal loans, and so on. (Should central banks act to restrict this? That is an interesting policy issue.)

This money market has been developing over centuries. It can work in any currency. Had Britain joined the Euro, the European Central bank would probably have set up in London: however the Eurocrats rely on expanding and developing European money markets. (Does one need all that many money markets? Might not one do for all of Europe? Or indeed for the whole planet? More fascinating policy issues.)

The heart of any large financial centre is its stock exchange. That runs side by side with the short-term money market, and the operations of the national debt. Money pumps through all these variegated systems like blood through arteries. As we have seen, the total amount of all this money seems ultimately to depend on the quantity of gold in existence. As I write, specialist firms have been spending large sums of money buying up gold in any form, (and more money still on their adverts). They were obviously expecting a future rise in the price of gold. And why? *Because world industrial capacity, particularly in Asia, is now increasing very rapidly.* Any time you are tempted to sell gold, dear reader, look at the world economic "conjuncture". Maybe you'll get more money if you *wait?* Or could you have a bit of fun telling the dealers you want more than they are offering?)

Any short-term limitation of the supply of money acts as a brake. As I write, Europe is not really sharing in world economic growth, nor is America, because both "economic unions" are applying such a brake. If other regions also applied the brake, this would tend to produce a sort of oscillation in growth rates. If that oscillation gets out of hand, could a recession result? That is what used to happen in the past. Oscillations used to develop and produce such large variations as to cause slumps, with bankruptcies, takeover bids, mergers, asset stripping and generalized stalling of growth in capacity. There would be less competition after the slump. Attempts to prevent this by controlling the money supply only made matters worse.

In the 1920s, following the German runaway inflation, central banks were (understandably) exceptionally nervous and probably overdid their attempts to stay "in control". The result was the 1929 world economic collapse, triggered by the collapse of a bank in Vienna and causing a blitz on the then over-optimistic New York Stock Exchange. The collapse did not affect the USSR, only because the Russian national capital was state-owned – the collapse only affected capital owned by "free enterprise" corporations. In a discussion at college in my undergraduate days, one left-wing student claimed that the Russians foresaw the crash.

It would be interesting to check the "opened" Soviet archives to see if this can be verified. Claud Cockburn, himself also left-wing, but very objective as a journalist, recorded in his biography a discussion he had with an American financial journalist who was extremely worried by the over optimism ; this was just before the storm his New York.

Certainly after 1929, the Russians claimed the crash as "proof" that the old way was doomed, and that the future was "in their hands". This attitude continued into the post-war period; it was presumably what Khrushchev meant when he said "we will bury you". But others saw different answers. Roosevelt set the "New Deal" in motion. And Hitler set the "New Order" on its march to Stalingrad. Hitler's war with Russia,

America's subsequent cold war with Russia and hot war in Vietnam, support for the "contras" in Nicaragua etc, were probably in the last analysis due to different "answers" to the problem posed by 1929. Could it happen again? Maybe. As I write it seems possible that the risk has been headed off. But the lesson to be learnt may be that a somewhat more "permissive" attitude to inflation may have to be struck. Which would mean that money would not then store value all that well. Perhaps we have an apparent paradox, namely the more that wealth and well-being increase, the greater the pressure on the "value" (subjective) of money ...

> If all producers get paid enough for their output, how is it then, if as consumers they don't have enough money to buy all the goods that have been produced?

6.12 Capital and the P.L.C.

If value is subjective, "cost" at first seems to be objective. It seems to be "fixed" by the productivity of each enterprise. But in fact it is still a price, and so a compromise between opposing valuations. It cannot be otherwise. Understandably, the owners of a company want a **money** return on their property. But real capital is ideas. If the ideas are getting to be time-expired, the **real** return is going to shrink, and perhaps even disappear altogether.

When I was at Fords, we were hitting the target money return on the money estimate of "assets employed". No doubt Ford, subsequently moved to Köln, still is. But this should reflect that money profit is a **residual** item out of money added value.

If capital is ideas, we have to bear in mind that no limited company or corporation can *think!* Its owners can think of course. It is natural that the entrepreneur should own the company s/he has created. Of course s/he should be free to bring in other shareholders if s/he wishes, but the usual reason for doing this is to finance expansion of capacity. If we are to have **engaged** ownership of companies, ownership which will turn companies round when they seem to be failing, it would really be better if some other way of financing for expansion were to be found. I happen to think that when a company is expanding its capacity, its purchases of extra assets should really be seen more as a cost, a cost to be

deducted from revenue *before* annual profit is struck!
This would mean that dividends would not be paid. An owner entrepreneur would not mind that – s/he would be focused on the longer term future.

But even the most engaged shareholders would object. This is why myself I believe that private companies are better for the overall economy, at least at first. They can be rather more dynamic. Moreover, in a private company, if the deficit went so far as to cause a loss, this could easily be financed by short-term borrowing. That of course, would scarcely do for a plc which has to be so mindful of its stock market "image".

Am I challenging established habits of mind too much? Maybe so, but I would counter that established habits of mind tend to be based on subjective valuations. Again, the money economy may be diverging here from the real economy. Some will no doubt object that if the company went to the stock market in the conventional way, it could raise additional money to speed up expansion. By sticking to self-finance, expansion might be slower? Perhaps, but the whole point of self-finance is that only the more dynamic companies can indulge in it. Dynamic companies can defer some of their expansion to next year, when further self-finance becomes available. And in subsequent years they will still be able to contemplate risks which the CEO of a plc would be unwise to take, since his own job would be on the line. And an even more fundamental point is that the self-financing private company may well be less prone to diverge from the real economy for excessively subjective reasons. That is the great advantage of keeping ownership solely in the hands of those who have created the company's capital ideas. Late incomers to ownership may not have such a clear grasp of these ideas. And that is what the *real* economy is about, like it or not.

It may be a pity that company law came into being before there were any economists. Company law is of course there to protect shareholders – but if the expanding private company can manage without shareholders, no such protection is necessary. It may also be a pity that government did not call Adam Smith in to advise them. Maybe they should have done, seeing that he had made his aversion to the embryo plc very plain. But 18th century politicians were not noted for their depth of understanding! Until something is done about all this, it should be carefully noted that accounting practice is based, quite understandably , on company law as it is, and perhaps falls away from company law as it should be.

In spite of the development of management accounting, it may still be the case that conventional practice tends to obscure the real economy.

May I again cite my experience at Fords. We were recruiting large numbers of people to staff the newly-established Central Finance function. Accountants didn't seem to be particularly useful! The man reputed to be our best departmental head, Bill Hayden, had no qualification at all! Another departmental head had a degree in history. He was thought to be the second best.

What made a department head good was his grasp of the real economy ...

6.13 Added Value.

Because of the division of labour, we have to have money. Because we have to have money, the added value (or net product) has to be shared out in money. Incomes of whatever kind can only come from added value. The total of incomes cannot exceed added value, not in a company taken separately, nor in the economy as a whole. Yet illogically enough, incomes are calculated without reference to added value. Wages and salaries are related to time. Interest and profit are calculated as percentages of money lent or invested. In this process, something has to be the residual item – and that is profit.

One man who attempted to propose a more logical system was Rudolph Steiner. His proposal has largely been ignored. Many economists are quite unaware that he ever made it, although it was published soon after the end of the First World War. He was the founder of the anthroposophist movement, and yet curiously enough neither of the two English translations made by anthroposophists, contain the sentence from his German text which puts it forward!

His proposition was extremely simple. Employers and employees should contract *in advance* to receive percentages of next years (or next months) added value. If added value increased, both "sides" would get more. If it contracted both would get less. It would be in the common interest for workers and employers to collaborate as closely as possible , more than they do at present. Steiner seems to have seen this as so blindingly obvious, that he did not trouble to enlarge upon it in his book. In the 1980s, the anthroposophist economist, Christopher Budd, did draw attention to it in his journal, but as far as I know, received little response.

Some years before I came across Steiner's proposition, when I was still at Fords, one of the Ford directors, J.M.A.Smith got interested in added value. He asked me to look at it, to get ideas for the next round of wage negotiations. As far as I know, no one had done this before. When I looked at the figures, I found that added value moved up and down all the time, with continual changes in stocks both of supplies and of finished products always occurring, day by day. This made the exercise hard to use in bargaining with the unions, but the thought did come to me then, that cumulative changes in one direction could reduce the pool of added value, perhaps quite suddenly. This might even be a factor in sudden bankruptcies, which do occur from time to time. In any event, the actual pool of money available to pay out incomes of all sorts varied so much more than the "standard cost" basis of Ford management accounting could highlight. When the added value tax was introduced some years later, this was probably the first time that any "call" on added value was related to how much of it there actually was. (No doubt professional partnerships must share out actual added value, but of course they do not have stock movements to blur the picture.)

Profit being a residual, only slight change in added value will have disproportionate impact on profitability. (That effect would of course be greatly reduced if Steiner's idea were tried out.) My observations at Fords were made month to month. Variations due to stock movements would presumably smooth out year to year, but that can only be calculated for sure *ex post,* at the end of the year and cannot be calculated *ex ante.*

If companies are owned by unengaged shareholders, temporary falls in profit often provoke them into selling out. But if an entrepreneurial sole owner could find a way of utilizing Steiner's idea in practice, s/he might find it very helpful, so long as the company was growing.

The workers would have every incentive to look for ways of increasing added value in their daily work. The eyes of management cannot be everywhere and shop floor workers often notice things ignored by managers. They have little incentive to do much about what they notice at present, but that could change if the practical difficulties of implementing this system could be overcome. Sharing out the added value in previously agreed percentages would focus everyone's attention on corrective measures *before* they were too badly needed. The snag would be that while employees would thus fare better in good times, their share will decrease uncomfortably in bad times while the rich owner can to some extent shrug off temporary reductions in income, the shop floor worker can't. S/he has fixed sums to pay out each month – rent or mortgage, health insurance, telephone bills and internet subscriptions. In spite of that, when I chanced to mention the idea of contractually sharing added value to Ernest Bader, the founder of Scott Bader, the reinforced glass fibre plastics people, that very impetuous entrepreneur immediately wanted a report done on it. So I did one for him. He was by then retired, and had long since taken the extraordinary step of giving his company to the people who worked there. So he wanted my report in enough copies to give to every member of the "Commonwealth". I arranged this. Ernest gave them I think to the company secretary to distribute. So enraged were the management that they siezed these copies and destroyed them!

This was done before the owner members even knew the report had been prepared. So Ernest paid me to post a new set of copies to each member's home address,(obtainable from the registrar of companies)! But, really, the management's doubts seemed to have been justified. Few members took the trouble to respond at all, and those that did were hostile. I could of course well understand this! Most company members would probably have had a mortgage! Ernest Bader, not only an archetypal entrepreneur, but also a quixotic idealist to boot, was not the sort of man to consider such details.

I did much later read a newspaper report that something of the sort was tried out in Romania under Ceausescu - and was so unpopular that it probably contributed to his blood stained downfall.

I had tried it out in a very small way in a job creation scheme, in typesetting for publishers. This was based in Ireland. and might have worked if we had not been "blacked" by the Irish compositors' union, so that the project had perforce to be abandoned. It might just possibly have worked if we had been able to grow quickly enough. We had no stock movements to contend with. So we might have been able to function in the same way as a professional partnership does.

In spite of all the possibly insurmountable difficulties in adopting Steiner's scheme, the problem it addresses still remains. Our way of sharing out added value might function better if it could be somehow more closely related to the pool of added value actually there. This might moderate inflation a little, and certainly make for improved relations between owners and employees. It would of course be easier to do if Henry Ford's dream of a high wage economy could be realized.

6. 14 Money and world economic balance.

The doctrine of comparative costs must, of course, work itself out through the medium of money. But if exchange rates are not at purchasing power parity, the results will diverge from the necessities of the world-wide real economy. It can be argued that this will correct itself in the long run, but this is only true to the extent that the long run brings about purchasing power parity, which is not necessarily likely when very large and self-contained regions enter into marginal international trade. In the long run we are all dead. If there is evidence of distortion of the natural real-economy pattern of world trade, the only possible remedy is that currencies which are overvalued should undertake very drastic devaluations, to go as far as possible towards correcting imbalances caused by what can be very considerable divergences in the international monetary system. These are probably the largest divergences between the money- and real economies on the surface of the planet.

For this reason, worldwide free trade is less important for economic development than regional free trade, particularly if the region is large enough and has or can establish a common currency. The initial beneficiaries of regional free trade are the poorer countries in the region, but the richer countries will begin to benefit once the poorer countries have had good growth for 3 or 4 years, and so can buy more of the richer countries products. If this seems to confine the benefits of comparative costs to particular regions, it will I think none-the-less be found that regional growth which is possible within the region is great. So great in fact as to bring speedier development on the whole planet, than would be the case if the fallacies engendered by monetary divergences are allowed to exert an excessive influence on the international monetary policies. Economists working for the World Trade Organization please note!

6.15 Illusion and Reality

The money illusion, that is the illusion that money is primary, when it is only secondary, tends to delude the rich more than anyone else. They put their money into loans, essentially because a loan which pays interest *seems* safer than investing in a new business, which of course entails obvious risk. Hence it is that "finance" looms so large in the current economy as I write. But unless the economy grows, the people who have borrowed the money find it hard to repay, and some default. This is what started happening in Europe soon after the new millennium began. It cumulated in a long-drawn out crisis, called rather mistakenly a financial one. It is really an entrepreneurial crisis. Not enough new businesses were being started up – a defect in the *real* economy.

All businesses go through a life cycle; every year some close down. So every year we need new ones starting up. We aren't getting them, not as I write. The money illusion leads to a wrong diagnosis. The crisis is said to have been caused by "over-lending". But it would be more to the point to say that it was caused by under-investment. Capital funds are useless if they are not put into new capital. It is really rather foolish for the rich to put their money into loans. where contrary to their beliefs, the risks may actually be greater ...

6.16 The financial problem.

There is seemingly an inexhaustible supply of loan-able funds for short and medium finance, but not enough risk investment to employ all the workforce. This is surely irrational. I believe that Adam Smith may have, in a way, foreseen this. Probably because he saw taking on a risk as a *good moral quality!* He was sceptical about the value of the "joint stock company" as the plc was then termed. His ideal was the rich man risking his own money. He saw that as the best way. It seems to me he had a point.

I am aware of large companies which were wound up when the application of good management techniques would have saved them – simply because the shareholders were not in the least way committed to "their" company. *Commitment* is the very least of entrepreneurialism. A very different example was furnished by the Ford Motor Company when the Edsel model was a disastrous flop. Henry Ford Junior was committed, and brought in the famous whizz-kids from Harvard, to turn the company round. They succeeded and the company is still with us as I write. Commitment can perhaps prolong the life of a company perhaps considerably. As winding up a large company usually involves the loss of a substantial base of assets, the economy which allows this to happen suffers grievously. For capitalism to be successful, it requires committed shareholder, as well as sound monetary management.

Committed shareholders may of course greatly increase capacity, and the money supply needs to be judicially increased *in pro rata,* with the increase in capacity. Such an increase is not at all inflationary; failure to arrange it can be disastrous.

Conclusion of this chapter

When I went up to the LSE in 1947, it was still a very young institution. Maybe this is why there was what I now suspect to have been a mistake in the way it was run? The mistake, if it was one, was simply that economics and money were taught as if they were two *separate* subjects. It wasn't as if anything wrong was taught – as I approach the end of my life, 62 year after I graduated I have come to the conclusion that I was far too critical of it when I was a youngster! Applying what I was taught, over my now quite long life, has made me respect it more and more. But the separation into *two* subjects of what can only be *one* subject might be the cause of the increasing *defectiveness* of academic economics; for it does seem to me as if economic dons now, in effect only teach the *second* subject.

But how can that be right? Real is primary, money is secondary. The real economy determines the money economy. It can't be the other way round. So if the monetary system, worldwide, is a bit warped, what one has to do is study the *real* economy to detect the degree of warping. The money economy can only be a mirror of the real economy.

We must always bear in mind that to the extent it is warped, to that extent it is beginning to become a distorting mirror.

Note; Maybe I should point out that I have not consulted any other book in writing **The Economics Quincunx.** On the contrary, everything I say derives from only two sources

a) my memories of what I was taught, 65 year ago as I write, and

b) my own practical experiences as a business economist in applying that, to me, hallowed teaching over my working life.

My experience as an economist is thus the reverse of David Ricardo's! Born in 1772, he had made a fortune in business by 1814. Three years later he wrote *the Principles of Political Economy and Taxation,* and then became an MP, active in the "free trade" movement. Whereas he wrote from the experience of *running* a business, I write from my experience of advising other businesses using among other sources, ideas Adam Smith and he were the first to develop. He entitled his book "Principles". I beg leave to doubt if there are really any principles in economics at all! The economy is a living human thing, and so beyond such academic niceties. There is the Quincunx. Only one of its 5 points is occupied by money, and events in the money system are produced by events in the other 4 points, and not the other way round.

Marx summarized Adam Smith and Ricardo, without really changing their system. He then used the analysis to propose his doctrine of exploitation, but that is a subjective value judgment, given plausibility only by the money system's divergences. In rebutting Marx, Jevons and others like him did not however escape from the monetary illusion. However by the time I was taught, people like Lionel Robbins were beginning to free themselves from it. I hope I have escaped from it completely, using only what I was taught. Whether I have succeeded is for others to judge, but if I have not, I feel certain that those who follow me will do so without difficulty,

7. ECONOMETRICS

Econometrics tends to demonstrate the crucial difference in economics, between *ex post* and *ex ante.* This is because econometrics has developed, over the last sixty years or so, by utilizing complex mathematical equations. Mathematics can only deal with what is quantifiable, and that primarily *ex post* .

Econometricians have little option but to *assume* that the mathematics will not change *ex ante.* Econometrics cannot take *qualitative* changes into account. I suspect that this is why economists failed to foresee the "crisis" which developed around 2008. This is not to say that econometrics is of no use. It can indeed be quite helpful in forecasting regular cyclical movement in the conjuncture. However we seem, as I write, not to be experiencing regular cyclical change, and I suspect the explanation will lie in *qualitative* factors.

The real economy is about real actions. For example; today in the whole planet an exact and finite number of packets of butter will be consumed. And the same sort of statement could be made about every single one of all the millions of commodities that exist. But such statements can only be correlated by a universal measure of some kind. Marx, drawing together the work of Smith and Ricardo, opined that hours of work constituted that measure. Is that so? It seems to me he totally ignores the *ideas* embodied in capital. There is also the secondary problem that his proposition cannot easily be made to allow for work of different skills. As we have seen, what actually happens is that *compromise* valuations are made, for example between the ideas of the entrepreneur and the hours worked by his "wage-slaves", or the hours needed with one skill as against another. Marx of course went on to say that what actually happens is not what *should* happen – but in doing so he went outside economics and into morality, so travelling in the opposite direction to Adam Smith's journey a hundred or so years earlier.

You can "worry" at the issue, like a dog worries at the bone, as long as you like (I have worried at it for 60 odd years) but you will surely come to the same ineluctable conclusion. Real actions in the real economy are objective; but any attempt to correlate them is *subjective.* Can it be otherwise? I think not. This remains so even when we content ourselves with the apparently tangible equivalent of money. "Money iss funny things". And econometrics can *only* work with money values, and they are all subjective.

On top of that, money itself is continually changing in value. It is a protean thing. And that is inevitable. That is what I mean when I say that the *real* economy is primary – real economic actions objectively occur – whereas their money reflection is secondary , being no more than the mosaic mirror of all the 7000 million people currently acting in the world economy. To think otherwise means elevating what each of us thinks about all these actions over the actions themselves. Which is plainly quite silly.

Some years ago the Queen of England asked why no one had foreseen the so-genannte "credit crisis". Is there such a thing? Real actions have confused our minds; such crisis as there is lies in our apparent inability to think about them. Two people thinking clearly about a valuation will not make the same valuation, but will at least be able to make a *workable* compromise between them. So multiply not thinking clearly 7000 million times and I suppose it does look a bit like a "crisis". But it is a crisis of *understanding* not of "credit".

Economists who did not realize that such a crisis could ever occur had not grasped that it could always happen at any time in any set of circumstances – *but only to the extent* that not enough of the 7000 million minds understood economics! Should we perhaps ask each of the 7000million minds to spend 2 or 3 years studying the subject and have them pass an examination! However if only twenty or thirty percent of the population passed, it would be enough to *adequately* influence all myriad compromises. Simply by those who understood telling the rest "No, that won't work", when *un*workable compromises were being put forward.

Short of such a "solution", economists who focused on *qualitative* factors ought to be able to detect a general "cultural" divergence of actual thinking from correct understanding of the economy. They might perhaps come up with a statement such as "we don't seem to have enough entrepreneurs". They might even come up with useful recommendations on ways of provoking people to become entrepreneurs.

There you are, your Majesty. It's not much of an answer to your question, but its the best I can manage. Maybe someone else can come up with a better one. But I suspect that someone will still have to focus on what is *qualitative* ... It does seem to me that academic economists should look critically at the curricula currently in vogue, and consider whether they focus sufficiently clearly on qualitative issues.

It does not seem to be generally realized, as I write, that econometrics can only measure money values. It can of course adjust to price changes, but that adjustment depends on the same package of goods being at least typically bought by consumers. Changes in this package do occur; nothing in the economy is free from change, beyond the basic need to work to live. And there may be little equivalence in the basic package of consumer necessities when monetary comparisons are made between different currencies. Such comparisons have continually to be made, somehow or other, in international currency markets.

Neither can econometrics cope very well with technological change, because it needs the boundaries between each sector of industry and the relative sizes of the various sectors to be "stable" - when technological change can and will make them very fluid. This can particularly affect the use of input/output tables, though in the short term they are probably good enough. Input/output tables would indeed be a valuable guide to short-term policy making, as was proposed by Professor Norm Stone, in his "Rocket" project at the Cambridge Department of Applied Economics in the early 60s. The idea got so far as leading to the formation of the N.E.D.O, but this was ignored by unusually stupid politicians.

Econometrics cannot digest the part played by ideas in the economic system. One cannot measure an idea. Econometrics has to see all the funds devoted to the implementation of ideas as if they were homogeneous stores of value, when they are anything but homogenous. Moreover more money spent does **not** denote better ideas. The Channel Tunnel cost much more because of the bigger bore required to take trains containing heavy goods vehicles, when a smaller bore tunnel taking only railway flat trucks carrying containers could have carried just as much traffic; and might even have been a better idea, given the "social" costs involved in coping with the resulting influx of HGVs on the British road network. As far as I know this point was not studied *ex ante* by the government.

Since econometrics can only treat with the money reflection of the real economy – a reflection which is by axiom imprecise, one has to look for monetary uses for it. Maybe the best use would be if it could calculate the increase in industrial capacity as it occurred, and do this sufficiently accurately to enable an exact enough increase in the money supply to be arranged. Unfortunately it is not very easy to know what the increase in capacity in any given period actually is. The increase planned by a given company as the expected result of a given increase in capital expenditure may not materialize exactly as forecast. There may be defects in the capital ideas involved. The quality of key supplies may not be entirely dependable. Construction may encounter unexpected difficulties in the terrain, notably with such things as tunnels, or perhaps because of unexpected subsidence. We live in an uncertain world. Even a highly sophisticated monetarist management may therefore be a little sceptical about the *ex ante* increase in capacity, and since the exact calculation of the necessary money supply is quite a fine balance, will probably tend to err on the side of caution - and therefore of deflation. This can of course mean that when the increased capacity has been successfully installed, it proves to be difficult to sell all the extra production now made possible.

Hence, the correct use of econometrics does require that sort of skilled judgement which can only result from years of experience. (One problem the European Central Bank faces is that it is a new situation entirely, of which no one has any experience at all.)

The use of econometrics by governments is now widespread. This is why I , as a business economist who has specialized in applying pure **theory,** have to sound so many notes of warning. It is widely understood that the whole apparatus of national economic statistics has no real basis in proper economic theory, simply because it presupposes that money reflects value. This can only be true **if** there is perfect competition – a text book assumption not often found in real life Oddly enough, econometrics does seem to readily "fit" with *Marxist* economics, at least if one disregards their view of the way their analysis establishes beyond doubt *massive exploitation.* It doesn't.

And even more strangely, econometrics shares with Marx an inability to take into account entrepreneurial ***motivation,*** a key factor!

I suspect that governmental agencies and politicians haven't grasped these *essential and inherent* limitations of econometrics. Econometrics applies very fancy algebraical equations to material drawn from government statistics. But obvioulsy enough government statistics do not - and generally speaking *cannot* record;

a) *the degree of competition* in each particular industry. By "degree" I refer of course to the wide range between oligopoly and textbook "perfect" competition.

b) the *entrepreneurial factor.* The true entrepreneur is a businessman/woman who sees and exploits the potential in something which has never been done before, or has always been done in some other way. No "figures" for *that!*

c) the *quality* of management. There is a very wide range here. In for example nationalized concerns, look at the difference between Volkswagen before privatization and (say) the US postal services! Private and public companies vary as widely.

d) *growth.* By the very nature of statistical recording, which simply agglomerates total figures over a time period – month, quarter or year, change as it takes place is averaged out. As statistics are not all that accurate, it is impossible to distinguish *real* change from accidental variations in accuracy – unless change is quite large. At present, such signs of recovery as are recorded are too small to be trusted much.

In any real situation, *effective* economic analysis should be more like 40% econometrics and 60% "judgment", ie *philosophical,* not mathematical at all. It isn't necessarily certain that any available set of mathematical equations can adequately deal with the monetary situation involved in growth.

In Britain, in the post war decades, there was full employment, and a will to invest among large companies, for example in the motor industry. However, the Bank of England and the Chancellor of the Exchequer repeatedly imposed restrictions on credit which would suddenly impact on growth. These restrictions were usually triggered by sudden increases in the adverse balance of payments. Expansion of car production necessitated more sheet steel; if the British steel industry could not expand its production of sheet steel, there would be a massive increase in imports. An increase in the adverse balance put pressure on the currency, and it was not thought desirable to devalue. The idea was conceived of developing the econometric analysis of input/output tables – which depict the money value of sales by each sector to all other sectors. The mathematical tool for this is vectors.

I was told on a visit to the Department of Applied Economics at Cambridge that they had not been able, at that time, to discover adequate mathematical equations to cope with the problem, and had to resort at least for a time to trial and error. The matter ceased to be important because the successive governments at that time lost interest in the input/output tables idea (which would have warned the steel industry to expand production *pari passu* with car production). And of course the development of the European project made it somewhat less important, as car production was moved from Britain to Germany (in the important case of Ford). I do not know if the "mathematics" were solved. No doubt they were, but only with a delay. Probably this sort of situation can recur from time to time.

The Propensity to Save.

A useful econometric analysis would be to check from time to time whether *in the currently prevailing circumstances* the propensity to save could not be usefully raised or in other words whether it is econometrically adequate. But in so doing it must always be borne in mind that the propensity is itself *qualitative* not quantitative, being based on subjective valuations of the value of saving as against the value of consumption. If these subjective valuations alter- as they can at any time – the propensity will have a qualitative tendency to change. These will of course have quantitative effects, but such as cannot be *econometrically* predicted.

CHAPTER 8. POLICY MAKING

Economics is philosophy. But philosophy is not just economics. Or so it would seem. Do you know how that is? I'm not sure I know either. Perhaps it is something someone ought to work on. If I live long enough I might have a go myself.

Meanwhile governments have continually to adapt economic policies. Or do they? Suppose we just let the economy run itself? Could that not be done?

These questions continually pose themselves. Probably they always will. *And as long as they do, policy makers will go on* mixing politics and economics – another philosophical question.

Any philosophy worth bothering with has to deal with *change.* Is change a thing that politicians *produce?* Or is it something they have to adjust to? Obama got elected on a slogan "Change we can believe in". Might "Change we cannot help" have been a better slogan? (The same question posed itself later with Francois Hollande's "Le changement, c'est maintenant". I saw an interesting programme on the Franco-German TV station Arte. It cheekily suggested that "Le changement c'est toujours" might have been better... This question underlies the whole of this chapter. The reader should bear that in mind.

Sometimes politicos try to prevent change – eg by regulation. Is that sensible? Is it even possible? And whatever the answers to these question are, economists have to *advise* politicos, that "if you do this, you will get so-and-so; but if you do that , you will get such-and-such". Which can get *complicated!* (Kipling said once "There are 960 ways of composing tribal lays and every single one of them is right". This seems to apply to economic policies.)

CASE STUDY; after the 1939 – 45 war, France and Germany pursued strikingly opposite monetary polices:-

a) Germany had a once-and-for-all currency *reform.* (It had a dramatic effect on consumption, notably on passenger rail travel)

b) France had successive *devaluations.*

However both countries had broadly similar growth rates during the 1950s.

Note; the French economist, Jaques Rueff, protested at the devaluations, saying that they made money "a lie". But it could be argued that it was just a matter of money being bad at forecasting its *future* value ...

Forecasting often misses out, not predicting quite important changes.

TWO CASE STUDIES:

1) No one forecast the Greek bankruptcy – for that is what it really was.

2) No one forecast the "financial" crisis. No less a person than the Queen of England asked why? To the best of my belief, no one has ever really answered her.

Let me suggest a possible answer to both. Forecasting is *conditional:* any forecast assumes that current policies are right, when they may be wrong!

Long before we had the complex econometric forecasting models currently in vogue, businessmen and economists watched for what were called lead indicators:-

a) A businessman in 19th century America is said to have watched the smoke coming from factory chimneys. If less smoke was coming out, less was being produced.

b) I myself found a simple lead indicator when I was working at the Bank of China.

I did a study on the price of tungsten as a "lead indicator" of a recession. My Chinese boss politely passed the study on to Head Office in Beijing, but I doubt if they were much interested. Hadn't they abolished the trade cycle? (Maybe they have – has Chinese economic growth yet had a trade cycle? Someone should do a study on that.)

In economics we are continually confronting the unknown. Sometimes we have to wonder if it is the unknowable! But governments still have to *do* things. Should we go back to protection – or not? Should we devalue – or should China revalue? We have endless economic "summits". What **answers** emerge from these summits? Politicos dare not admit it, but *they don't know what is going on.* Economists can't take that attitude! When I was at Fords in the 60s, the National Institute of Economic and Social Research had a warning on the back cover of their journal, that the workings of the economy were "imperfectly understood". Perhaps they still think like that. But to me that way of putting it suggests they hadn't thought things through. I myself suspect they had too much faith in econometrics. Why do I see it that way? I suspect they kept finding that their economic analyses didn't give them *correct* forecasts. But instead of focusing on the fact that econometrics doesn't work, they came to the conclusion that some mysterious unknown factors were throwing their calculations out! Probably the true reason was that they were out of touch with the *divergence between the real economy and its money reflection.*

Many of the economists involved were mildly left wing. To them, the entrepreneur was a fiction, invented by right wing economists to deflect criticism of the capitalist system. So they ignored what was called micro-economics, which has to focus on the entrepreneur, and switched over to macro-economics which focuses on *money* totals, like the GNP, the total of capital investment expenditure in money terms, the total money value of exports and imports; all that sort of thing. They felt *safe* there. But, you see, real capital is **qualitative.** You can see how much money has been spent on capital. But that doesn't tell you whether what you are getting is much good or not.

They believed - and I suppose many econometricians still do – that if in two or three successive years, the same percentage of the money GNP goes on capital expenditure, there will be the same *result.* This simply isn't so.

How good the result is depends on the *quality* of the investments. One can perhaps attempt to judge the quality *ex ante,* but only up to a point. One has to get down to specifics. The Russian 5-year plans in the thirties tried to do that. I was very disappointed when I went to the London School of Economics in 1947. The railways had just been nationalized. *I was childishly keen on railways.* I still am! In the pre-war period, the railways had been getting into deeper and deeper financial problems. Although they made some superb locomotives – for example, the Greesley Pacifics. But each of the four main railways made *different* locomotives. Wouldn't it be better in a small island if they *standardized*? That's what I thought.

So I went up to university expecting that the economics lecturers there would tell me how we must now manage *one single* railway organization for the whole country. But the lecturers weren't at all interested in *specifics, only in rather distant* abstractions ...

CASE STUDY; In 1945 the Russians must have been misled by the seeming success of their 1930s economy. They failed to understand that this success was due largely to Lenin and Stalin farming the economy out to entrepreneurs. Not all the Russian communists had agreed with this, even in the 1920s. After the tremendous victory of 1945, these dissidents seem to have agitated for a truly "socialist" economy in the Soviet corridors of power. Stalin, who was probably poisoned, was then rubbished by Khrushchev. The latter then boastfully told the Western World, "We will bury you". For a time it seemed to be working. Much to the astonishment of the Americans, the Russians got their first man into space. But towards the end, Gorbachev was pleading with the Americans to abandon their so-called "Star Wars" plan. *The Russians could not afford to match it!* The command economy simply did not work. It was based on *abstractions* not specifics.

The Soviet economy began to stagnate. The methods of the 1917 revolution had worked only in a very *unusual* situation. The grotesquely incompetent Tsarist regime had simply and totally collapsed. *There was anarchy.* Everyone slangs Lenin for seizing power – but could any less repressive regime have really tackled the problem? Maybe – maybe not. On one occasion a station- master down the line from Moscow was flagrantly disobeying orders. Lenin sent a squad of soldiers down to the station; they summarily shot the station-master on his own platform. Rough! What would an attempted democracy have done? The railways had to function. City populations were nearly starving. Food had to be brought in.

The economy slowly restarted.

Yet Europe in its bumbling way has still contrived to imitate Khrushchev by installing a stultifying bureaucracy!

My aim as an economist is to put MacDo's out of business. If every government and business just followed the simple and indeed eternal teachings in this textbook, we would fairly soon all be so rich, that we would eat at restaurants where the chef was not only an individualist but also a consummate artist.

NOTE; to shareholders in MacDos. Dont sell your shares yet! No need to worry at all! Boneheaded governments obstinately and tenaciously cling to demonstrably stupid economic policies. These ridiculous policies do not even do much good for the wealthy oligopolistic vested interests that spend so much time, money and sheer effort lobbying politicians, shareholders, oligopolists – and all other citizens. Read on. All we need to do, all of us, is to modify our attitudes. Which however we won't do, because we all cling pigheadedly to our conflicting *opinions*. The founder of anthroposophy, the Austro-Croatian Rudolph Steiner held that there were only twelve opinions – all of which were barriers to understanding. Applied to economics, he seems to have had a point.

Opinions are held by *interests;* all economic deals have (axiomatically) to be compromises *between conflicting interests!* The whole point about competition is that is provides the infrastructure necessary for *sensible* compromises to be negotiated. Try and get an oligopoly to compromise anything! Oligopolies successfully persuade governments to obstruct compromises by needless and silly *regulations,* coupled with idiotic policies. These produce stagnation, ossification and then degeneration of the economy. Dear Soviet Union, we are following you! These policies are presented to the citizens as if they were the only policies possible! Up to about 2006, the politicians could get away with that. But then it started to come unstuck. The policies were seen to fail. Most of Asia and Brazil too were doing much better. Why?

This ought to have been *predictable.* As indeed the Queen of England concluded! She broke her constitutionally-requisite silence to ask *why* the gathering crisis had not been foreseen.

Did anyone give her an answer? After a deafening silence from *academe,* I belatedly and hesitantly wrote to her. Without going into any detail with her, I suggested that university economic faculties up and down the country ought to *review* their curricula. Are they teaching economics properly? She kindly passed my letter on to the Prime Minister. This is the reply I got.

10 DOWNING STREET
LONDON SW1A 2AA
www.number10.gov.uk

From the Direct Communications Unit

9 August 2012

Mr David Columba Green
47 Rue du Pont Lottin
62100 Calais
France

Dear Mr Green

I am writing on behalf of the Prime Minister to thank you for your letter and enclosure addressed to Her Majesty The Queen, which has been passed to this office by Buckingham Palace.

It is good of you to get in touch. Mr Cameron very much appreciates your taking the time and trouble to inform him of your views.

With best wishes.

Yours sincerely

Correspondence Officer

The reader will notice that the acknowledgement fails to say whether the Prime Minister was going to actually *do* anything at all to address the point. *But shouldn't he?* The Queen's question seems to call for *action* of some sort. The Prime Minister's masterly inactivity is really rather worrying.

Continually over the years, we have had economic advice to governments falling short of what is needful. Economic policies so very often don't work out at all. Shouldn't that be looked into? What is the point of funding university economics faculties when nothing very useful for the country as whole results?

8.1 Why don't economic policies work?

If economic theories are in themselves wrong, no policy based on them is ever going to work! Isn't that so? It won't matter how "good" the government is! It won't matter how "esteemed" the economic advisers are! If the basic "pure" theory isn't adequate, *error is built in* - before the "esteemed" expert got his very first job in his undergraduate years ...

All my now long lifetime, this has been for me like St Paul's thorn in his side. I now feel I have been very slow on the uptake! Because in writing this book, I have come back, quite ineluctably, to just a *restatement* of the eternal truths of pure economic **theory,** as I was taught them in 1947-50**.** If the theory is now wrong, we will get **applied** nonsense. That is surely what has been happening. I think the theory in this book is right. That's not boastful at all. I'm just restating what the great masters of the past said. Read them yourself if you dont believe me.

CASE STUDY; The Greek Bankruptcy. The concept of bankruptcy is really pretty elementary! It is as old as the free market economy itself. All economic actions involve *risk.* If things go sufficiently wrong, the bills can no longer be paid. This applies to countries as well as to companies. (It happened to Germany in the1920s.)

It is not particularly my opinion that it happened, as well, to Greece. The head of Germany's Commerzbank said as much when the crisis started. The hapless attempts to "bail Greece out" have since showed that he was right! The huge loans since made will probably never get fully repaid.

Commerzbank as an important bank in Europe's largest creditor country would have had enough of the figures available to make a sound judgement. *There should now be an investigation into how the supposedly "expert" International Monetary Fund failed to see what was obvious.*

(It rather looks as if its chief, Dominique Strauss-Kahn, had his mind on other things.)

I think we can dismiss newspaper comment that it was "necessary" to pour money down the drain "to save the Euro" (!) The Euro was safe enough.

Example; *A few years earlier a very large American company went bankrupt, but the dollar was unharmed!* Probably it was as big as Greece. The essence of bankruptcy is that foolish *lenders* have to lose as well as the foolish *borrowers.* Banks might have gone under. No doubt the banks pleaded for the course that was adopted. But the figures are surely too greatly adverse for that justification to wash! And if both borrowers and lenders lose, the effect on the currency is pretty well *zero*; it cancels out.

If the whole European establishment, the European Central Bank, and the International Monetary Fund don't understand a simple idea like bankruptcy, we are all going to face an uphill struggle getting their bony heads around somewhat more involved concepts - such as the *inadequacies* of econometrics! (I repeat: no *econometricians* foresaw the Greek bankruptcy, any more than they foresaw the "financial" crisis which immediately preceded it.) Any readier of this book should now be able to see the *flaw* in it. The establishment no longer understands the *divergence* between the real economy and its money reflection!

The real *economy* is all about work. When one is bankrupt, one has to *work* one's way out of it! Everyone in Greece, rich or poor, should now be working like crazy to solve *their* problem. Yet the "solutions" imposed by the foolish "establishment", in its blindness, have actually caused a *massive rise in Greek unemployment!!!* Need I say anymore? Isn't that completely crazy! People who are able to work should always be able to find work, crisis or no crisis. That's how any crisis gets solved. The catastrophic German defeat in 1945 was followed by a *Wirtschaftswunder,* brought about by *work. The Greek bankruptcy should have had the same result* - and surely would have done if the *fact* of bankruptcy been addressed ...

The living complexity of any and every economy has to be allowed to pursue its own natural course: *even if that course leads to bankruptcy.* In its continuing development over time, the economy is shaped by forces which *cannot* be controlled by governments. These forces are the inexorable result of all the myriad human actions in the economy. Every living human takes economic actions every single day in *consuming*; and the majority of adult and all able people take economic actions in their daily work. Governments cannot possibly decree how this vast and indeed mysterious complexity has to function in the way they might like. As happened with the former USSR, the European economy has *stagnated.*

As I write, it is now in ongoing crisis. *This should have been foreseen!* (That is the point of the Queen's question!) It would have been foreseen! Europe's governing wiseacres should have taken the trouble to *learn* from the Soviet failure! The lesson from history is that those who will not learn from it are doomed to repeat it.

If you, the reader, wonder whether the Soviet example is irrelevant because they had total nationalization, whereas Europe has private companies, let me just point out that over-large oligopolistic companies are at least as rigid as nationalized ones. Having had some experience with both nationalized monopolies and oligopolistic multinationals, I myself wonder whether the latter are not in fact even worse! But it is enough to prove the point that so much of Europe's industry is now just as ossified as Soviet industry was. That's why, as I write, we have **crisis.**

What to do?

The first thing to grab is that unemployment is *avoidable.*

CASE STUDY; Between 1939 and the mid 1970s Britain had full employment. If you don't believe me, check the statistics out.

So why on earth don't we copy what was done then? Are we completely crazy? What does unemployment do?:-

- it **increases** government expenditure
- it **decreases** government revenue from income tax.

Policy makers who can't see even that are *incompetent*. It is they who should be sent to the back of the queue for jobs … We have stagnation because there is not enough competition. Short-term emergency measures may be needed to get people back to work – perhaps a return to protection would give us a breathing space. But we will still need to re-establish competition.

If there are too few companies, there *cannot* be enough competition and there will also be unemployment. The solution to both problems is the same. We need more **new** companies to compete with the existing ones. European Union policy makers claim to be "concerned" about competition. Let me comment with a gloriously mixed metaphor. They are both looking through the wrong end of the telescope and putting the cart before the horse. European policy seems to pose the question in the wrong form: "How can Europe protect competition from being interfered with?" This is not the right question, nor can it be for years to come. Before we can protect competition, don't we need to establish it? Turn the telescope round! Look through the right end.

In many industries, there is no longer all that much competition to protect. In others, competition is being destroyed by the tendency towards oligopoly. *Abstract* regulations do not distinguish between oligopolies and the new, still smaller firms that must compete with them. So we have regulations which, if purporting to maintain competition, in practice have the *opposite* effect! Put the horse before the cart! Competition is the only horse that can pull the European economic cart out of its present immobility.

Let's get back to competition first. I'm tempted to say, lets get back to *capitalism*! Looking at swollen oligopolies, some of which have been in existence for several generations, is this still capitalism at all? We need a *strong* competitive horse to drag the economic cart back towards still more competition, that is "back to the future". We need *growth!* Only in growth can new companies start up and flourish. Europe needs a new Wirtschaftswunder, this time for *all* 27 member nations, not only the original six.

This involves *specifics*. *Specific* new companies must be created, different from existing companies, with *specific* new products, not at all necessarily "high tech" products, but highly *marketable*. That needs *imagination*. Imagination is the key thing. Imagination means entrepreneurs. Only entrepreneurs can turn imagination into reality. What makes a successful entrepreneur is not quantity, but quality – how brilliant are his ideas?

The best entrepreneurs imagine something *that has never been done before*. This year's new entrepreneurs are the cutting edge of next year's growth. If we haven't got much growth this year, that means we didn't have enough entrepreneurs last year. Policy makers need to find out *why*! We must be obstructing entrepreneurs somehow – probably by all these fuss-pot regulations.

8.2 Policy and Imagination

Governments have to address the connections between economic change and imagination. Are their own policies sufficiently imaginative in themselves? Shouldn't policy makers imagine a better economy before they try to nudge real economic actors towards it? And there seems to be a mal-distribution of imagination between various sectors of the private economy

CASE STUDY; a TV advert.

A scantily clad and nubile young lady gets up in the morning. She discovers she has a sore throat.

The bright idea occurs to her of taking a patent branded medicine which is claimed to alleviate the symptom. She is attractive and the ad is quite compelling. But wait a minute! In real life, if I have a sore throat, don't I just go to the chemists and buy medicine. *Why does it need to be advertized at all?* TV advertizing is expensive. Why do pharmaceutical companies spend money on it. Because the branded product the advertisement promotes *costs more* than its "ethical" equivalent. The ad is not to tell us about a better product – but to con us into paying more for the *same* product. That is how oligopolies carry on.

This need not be! Why not second the imaginative ad men to the pharmaceutical company's research lab? A new mind, asking different questions, can open the doors of thought to new *ideas.* New technologies come up all the time. Sore throats are caused by viruses. Here in France, the sore throat virus has, it seems, *mutated.* Sore throats seem to be different in recent years. Maybe we can kill the mutated virus more easily in a new way? I have seen it suggested that nano-technologies might be able to combat viruses. That is the sort of question a new mind could ask – particularly a new mind *with imagination.*

But what can mere government policy makers do to help this approach. They could perhaps restrict or discourage certain types of advertizing. If policy makers also use i*magination*, they can maybe think of policies which will shift the focus of management attention to **new** ethical products. We could even curtail television advertizing quite savagely. After all, its largely there to help oligopolies push expensive goods. In particular, we could ban all advertizing of medicaments. The pharmacists are there. They can give people all the objective advice needed. (Pharmacists are of course small businesses.) Moreover cutting advertizing back would drive a lot of imaginative minds out of advertizing. Where would they go? Maybe some would become entrepreneurs.

Of course, many oligopolies do employ an economist or two. These study forecasts. But again, wait a moment. If the official national forecast for the coming year is low, then the oligopoly's economist will advise their CEOs to go easy on growth this year! But wait a moment. Suppose the oligopoly *ignored* the forecast, and went all out for growth, what would happen?

The oligopoly is large enough to spark enough purchases from suppliers *to change the forecast!!!* Any economic forecast based on econometrics can all too easily be what is called a "self-justifying hypothesis". Poor growth forecasts actually cause what happens. They make oligopolies act in such a way as to produce the result predicted!

Entrepreneurs don't bother with such forecasts much. They are too busy *imagining* things which can't be forecast! They don't move with the crowd. (They aren't even able to!) People often think entrepreneurs a bit stupid. But they are really just *different.* They don't forecast the future. *On the contrary, they make it.* No two people can share the same imagination. That is the reason why entrepreneurs act *on their own.* They can of course attract "loyal helpers". But when an entrepreneur is in charge there can be no "joint" decision making!

Which is why even loyal helpers sometimes find they are in disgrace! Entrepreneurs are "difficult". Outsiders often find them "impetuous" or "irrational". But no entrepreneur has time to *explain,* let alone "convince"! Each step s/he takes is in pursuit of their own dream. If his imagination is truly creative, it works! But his way of doing things *cannot* be changed! (even if it fails.) Either it succeeds, or it fails; but only the one person can steer the ship – either into harbour or else onto the rocks. NB*;* This is utterly unlike what second-phase *management* has to do. The second phase management team don't use imagination all that much. Their task boils down to a cyclical movement between the four management roles:-

- setting targets
- measuring performance against targets
- developing corrective measures to shortfalls
- making the team apply the corrective measures all utterly unlike the entrepreneur's methods!

Entrepreneurs are always needed. There is always change. Change always needs a new approach. Second-phase managers have only their pre-set cycle of tasks, which tick over repetitively like the strokes of an internal combustion engine. *Boring!* But they are necessary to keep their mostly *static* companies in the black.

When the entrepreneur dies or retires, he won't normally find another like him. Bernard Shaw addressed this very problem in his play *Major Barbara.* The entrepreneur character, Andrew Undershaft is brilliantly sketched. He has a theatrical solution to the problem of succession: he will not have anyone from his own family. They are all second-phase minded. So in Shaw's play, Undershaft *upsets* them all by saying he will leave it to any "foundling" he can find.

It *might* work. Perhaps one day an entrepreneur will actually try it.

OWNERSHIP CASE STUDY; Scott Bader.

Ernest Bader, a Swiss, came to England because, as a pacifist, he wished to avoid military service. He had a knowledge of the chemical industry, and to support himself he developed a small business importing and exporting chemicals. That was just after the end of the First World War. By the time the Second World War had started he was running a small but growing factory employing several hundred people, manufacturing fibreglass plastic. After the war it continued growing. At the age of 55 he retired. However he did not sell the business. He *gave* it to the people who worked with him – the people who had helped to build it up. This has often been presented as a piece of unparalleled generosity. I don't think, myself, that it was. It could be seen simply as recognition of the fact that they had built it up with him. It was as much their company as his. His *function* as the entrepreneur did not morally make him the sole owner. It wasn't as if he had started with a large sum of money of his own. The business had grown by self finance. He had never as far as I know borrowed money to build the business. The business had grown by virtue of his *ideas* on plastics. Legally, the business was his, and his son's, when they jointly "gave it away". But the question poses itself. Does the legal concept of company ownership, as we have it, reasonably reflect the real economy? Arguably not in this case, might one say? As I have mentioned, it isn't as if he had started with a large sum of money and used that to buy the machinery, laboratories and materials needed to get going. Should it become government policy to see ownership as somehow broadening out to the extent that there is self finance? If wages are really a sort of share in profit, might that be right? As an economist, I cannot answer. It is an example of how policy *could* go beyond the economic sphere

8.3 Regulation

All regulation hampers imagination. The bureaucrats who draft regulations do not understand that the world is continually changing. So they do not even attempt to imagine where the future is going. Whereas entrepreneurs do little else! No wonder bureaucrats and entrepreneurs are endlessly in conflict!

Far from imagining the future, the bureaucrats try to tie the future down to the past. Though regulations can only apply *ex ante,* they are inevitably constructed out of *ex post* beliefs. By the time a regulation is finally drafted and instituted, it has already lost touch with endlessly changing reality! Entrepreneurs who have to do something new find they are *obstructed.* The essence of regulation is to demand that everything is done exactly as it was in the past! That is the last thing the real economy actually needs!

Just as different animals in an ecology survive by being *different*, and by having evolved different modes of survival, so likewise, different entrepreneurs diversify in every imaginable way.

The boneheads in (for example) Brussels have drafted an enormous European regulations mountain. They know nothing of that diversity! Instead the witless fools try to have the same uniform regulations throughout the extremely diverse European Union! The very fact that they have this aim is in itself proof of their incompetence. We would be best placed with zero regulation. But if governments cannot yet be got to see sense, there should be at least totally different regulations in each different country!

CASE STUDY; South African bank charges.

Below is a reply I received when I protested about the *exorbitant* charges being levied in South Africa just for issuing a banker's draft in another currency. (These charges are to be noticed all over the world, not only in South Africa.) What happened was that Jewel Koopman, curator of a South African library, set up especially to collect books in the bad old days of apartheid, wanted a copy of a book I publish, **Nqonqotha,** by Anthony Barker, a medical missionary who had devoted his whole life to South Africa. The point to note is that the regulatory body was *totally unable* to address the problem that all available banks made much the same excessive charge. A *useless* and *pointless* regulator!

South African Reserve Bank

FROM THE OFFICE OF
THE REGISTRAR OF BANKS

CONFIDENTIAL

Ref: DIA7191g

2004-09-30

Mr D Green
Maoildearg
47 Rue du Pont Lottin
62100 Calais
FRANCE

Dear Mr Green

COMPLAINT REGARDING BANK CHARGES

Your letter dated 31 August 2004 refers.

The Office for Banks derives its authority, rights and powers from the Banks Act, 1990 (Act No. 94 of 1990 - hereinafter referred to as "the Act"). In view of the fact that the Act confers no authority upon this Office to interfere in matters concerning a bank/client relationship, and this Office, therefore, cannot involve itself in such a relationship, the mediatory role that this Office can play in disputes arising from a bank/client relationship is limited. Complaints of this nature that are received are normally sent, under cover of a letter from this Office, to the chief executive officer of the bank concerned, with the request that the dispute be resolved directly with the client. Furthermore, the bank concerned is requested to furnish this Office with a copy of its response.

Since, in this instance, we have not been furnished with the name of the relevant bank, we are not in a position to follow the procedure outlined above.

We also wish to advise that an ombudsman has been appointed, specifically to investigate complaints against banking institutions.

The Ombudsman for Banking Services may be contacted at the following address:

Adv N Melville
Ombudsman for Banking Services
P O Box 5728
JOHANNESBURG
2000

PO BOX 8432 PRETORIA 0001 • 370 CHURCH STREET PRETORIA 0002 • SOUTH AFRICA • TELEPHONE (012) 313-3911 • TELEFAX (012) 313-3758

The huge European regulations mountain is far and away the worst case of swollen government on the surface of the planet. There are ***millions of pages*** of opaque directives couched in grotesque jargon.

Why?

We have forgotten why the European project was started!

In the early 1950s, productivity comparisons were made between Europe and the U.S. In these comparisons, it was found that American Productivity levels were far higher than European ones. This was attributed, probably correctly, to the higher *economies of scale* obtaining in America. They were higher because the U.S. had a large single market and a single currency. Whereas every European nation had its own currency and tariff walls against imports.

All that was needed was to abolish the Intra-European tariff walls and merge the currencies into one. This second requisite took many years, but as I write we have now had a single market for two decades, and a nearly single currency for one. That has as I say taken an inordinately long time to achieve. *But now it has been achieved, the ensuing results are pathetic!* Instead of growth we have stagnation. We should have had a runaway boom throughout the European Union. All that has happened is good growth in one or two countries eg Poland, but the rest stagnate.

Why has this happened?

The E.U. institutions in Brussels should by now have initiated a major study to find out why!

They haven't bothered!

Seemingly, they haven't even realized that the last 20 years have been a bitter disappointment and failure. (For me as an economist it is the worst disappointment of my life.)

But the bureaucrats are so monumentally stupid that they haven't even grasped the nature, the sheer magnitude, of the problem. Instead they have toiled often into the small hours of the night drafting all these senseless, indeed ridiculous regulations. All that need ever have been done was to sign a simple treaty, in which all the signatories agreed not to discriminate against each other's businesses, with free movement of goods, funds and people in one single Common Market. (The term "Common Market" was adequately defined in the old General Agreement on Tariffs and Trade (G.A.T.T)) If left to itself this might have worked. It in fact needed little "policing". GATT did provide some leverage against breaking the rules, and each country would have known that if they broke the rules they would face retaliation. Everyone stood to gain by sticking to the treaty.

So why have these bureaucracies at all? They cost an enormous sum, and they do nothing useful. Instead they *stifle* entrepreneurs. We should abolish the European Commission immediately. Any problems which emerged could be dealt with by the *accountable* European parliament. Apart from that the only "governance" the European Union needs is that of the European Central Bank (which needs to be better run, a point I shall return to)

It is obviously the Regulations Mountain which is hampering new entrepreneurs, and so causing stagnation. Why I say this is because it is **axiomatic** that entrepreneurs do *not* need encouragement! (If they need encouragement, they are not entrepreneurs!) So there are the following things which need to be done, all of them, *urgently*:-

1) De-regulate
2) De-regulate
3) De-regulate
4) De-regulate
5) De-regulate

....

Will the reader please imagine this list continuing at least 100,000 times! Because that's how many stupid "directives" there are. Eurocrats might argue that consumers "need protection". But it is consumers who know what protection they need! Let us make it easy for them to get it.

CASE STUDY; I was supplied a golf-ball IBM composer (used for book texts) which repeatedly threw up badly spaced letters, ruining the work. The IBM engineer finally traced the fault. It took him a whole afternoon to fix it. I took the trader to the small claims court. The trader, myself and an arbitrator (in effect) sat and talked for about 20 minutes. The result was I was awarded a reasonable sum. (I did not have to pay a lawyer.)

If all Europe had simple easy-access courts (like the small-claims courts in Britain) to which consumers could speedily take complaints, and obtain compensation, would there still be need for regulation?

NB these courts would however need to deal purely with questions of fact. They would need to be prevented from considering points of law. They would not hear lawyers at all! There would be no need. But once legal precedents are allowed in, silly miscarriages can take place.

CASE STUDY; I had a few hundred books printed by a book printer, Halstan. But the printer delivered them to someone else, the author instead of me. I refused to pay Halstan's bill. Their lawyer advised them to go to court. *I believe the Halstan executives I deal with were embarrassed by this*, (from their shy behaviour when the case was heard.) They could not deny they had given them to someone else. Their lawyer claimed that they were entitled to consider that the author had "ostensible authority" to take the books. Halstan executives knew perfectly well that this was nonsense. An author has *no* authority to take the publishers goods! Yet believe it or not, the court ordered me to pay! I appealed. But the appeal judge listened while I explained about "ostensible authority" – and then upheld the first courts order!. I had to pay! Needless to say I never used that printer again!)

Such easy access courts must apply a *simple* code for small transactions. Laws which might apply to *large* companies should not be applied in these courts. Such a bar is easy to devise; "ordinary" courts would refuse to hear a defence against claims below a certain amount. If that were done, we could dispense with regulations claimed to protect consumers. NB; Are these claims justified?

To sum up on regulations, what I am saying is really simple enough. Every regulation in every country on the surface should be scrapped. We should only have laws, the texts of which should be carefully worked out by *accountable* elected representatives. If the laws are not quite clear and need interpretation that is a matter for the courts. That is what courts are for. Continuing interpretation is established by precedents. The interpretation of laws is absolutely not a matter for the executive to poke its interfering nose into. It is because a whole culture of executive interference has swollen to idiotically monumental proportions that we have such ludicrously high taxes. The penalty for letting this state of affairs continue can be seen from history. This is what sank the good ship Soviet Union, which could, *had it only returned sensibly to free enterprise capitalism,* been still afloat today. It is utterly astonishing; really it is, that this historical lesson has still not penetrated through the thick skulls of those who run the European catastrophe – the so called Commission,

8.4 Function and Ownership

The entrepreneur has a function which only s/he can perform. He will have a unique vision. So he will normally have to use his own money. Precisely because his visions and idea are unique, no one else will easily understand him well enough to *finance h*im! However it is possible, though not necessarily desirable, for him to perform the *function* without having *ownership.* This has on rare occasions happened: it might possibly be done more often in some very specific situations.

CASE STUDY; Soviet capitalism, 1917 – 1939.

The French academician, Helene Carriere d'Encausse has written an interesting biography of Lenin. She found that when he seized power, the factory workers and their trade unions, wanted to *own* the factories. Lenin refused point blank. All he would give them was a voice in running the factory. A broadly similar idea applies in France today.

So Russian factories, for most practical purposes, went on being managed in much the same way as before 1917. However the top manager might have been an enthusiastic communist. But even if he was, he would have been able to behave as if he was an entrepreneur. *There were no longer any owners to tell him what to do.*

This system was formalized as the "New Economic Policy". The results were fantastic. Example; a huge new industrial complex was built near iron ore deposits at Magnitogorsk, beyond the Urals. There was in fact a pre-war Soviet Wirtschaftswunder. Simply because it was so much like entrepreneurial capitalism. Note however that the "entrepreneurs" did not get high monetary rewards. I imagine that their motivation was patriotic – Tsarist Russia had suffered a catastrophic defeat. But for Lenin's brute force, the country would have been over-run by Germans, English and Japanese. Everyone was afraid this would recur – and of course in 1941 it did. So there was great enthusiasm for developing military power that would match the Germans.

Be that as it may, it is still a fact, that function was separated from ownership. Can this separation be usefully copied at all, in other circumstances?

I suspect there might be occasions when similar separation could be looked at, so as to get the vital uplift of the entrepreneurial spirit, perhaps to rejuvenate a business of the point of failure. Temporary leasing of a near bankrupt business to an entrepreneur might still turn thing around, perhaps by leasing the company to him for a long enough period. He need not own the company. He would just need a free hand.

Here are two cases which occur to me:-

1) Companies which would otherwise be wound up, with the loss of the value of the shares. These could be *leased* to any entrepreneur willing to put money into turning the company round, on terms that would enable him to make a substantial

profit. Once he had turned it round, and made his profit, it could revert to shareholders.

2) Companies which don't show much profit, but still earn enough added value to pay salaries and service loans have often been the subject of management buy- outs. Their problem may be that second-phase managers don't, generally speaking, have the dynamism of the true entrepreneur. There might be various deals by which they could bring an entrepreneur in.

CASE STUDY; A.E.I.

In the mid 50s, my former director at Fords, John Barber was given the job of turning A.E.I. round, and made its finance director. He took on people who had worked with him at Fords. (Many people had left English Ford when resources were switched to Ford of Cologne – at that time on the other side of the early Common Market tariff wall.)

One of John Barber's ex-Ford aides was Derek Whittaker, who was later to go to British Motor Corporation. Derek knew me and got me to organize a short business course, with a business game for A.E.I. executives. The idea was to alert them to the sort of financial planning (really *economic* planning), which had been used at Dagenham. I do believe this would have worked. But A.E.I. shareholders lost their nerve - and sold out to G.E.C. a rival concern in the heavy electrical industry. The British economy lost out!

Had there been effective legislation to restrict such take-overs – which *diminish* competition – A.E.I. could have been saved. The way to do it would have been to have leased the company out to John Barber, not as Director of Finance, but as entrepreneur, a role I think he could have fulfilled. He would have carte blanche until the company was turned round, and when it had been he should have been rewarded by shareholding and appointment as second-phase CEO, with the rest of the ownership and control restored to the other shareholders.

As it was, G.E.C. did not do all that well out of the deal. Arnold Weinstock, the CEO of G.E,C, expected to get A.E.I. technical experts to work for him. This did not happen: they all lived in Kent, and did not want to move to the Midlands! Rather than that they got other jobs. I was told some of them got posts as bank mangers – their real expertise being *thrown away*! I was also told that plans for a new high-tech type of telephone exchange were thrown in the furnace, rather than let Weinstock have them. The British heavy electrical industry was thus weakened, and economic growth was less than it could have been. Such can be the nefarious effects of short-termist take-over bids. Policy makers should encourage different approaches.

It would be much better for all of us if companies in difficulties were turned around in this way if at all possible. This would still be worth while, even if a company was making no profits at all, as long as it could for a period keep going. A further refinement could be to motivate despondent employees. Surely a restoration of company morale would make an important contribution, perhaps a decisive contribution, to recovery. What I would suggest is something along the lines of the following, for which suitable enabling legislation could clear the way generally.

I would think it might be a good idea to make senior employees, indeed why not all employees, shareholders in the company. It would then have share divided into two classes, voting and non-voting. The same dividend would be paid on both classes, but, at least for a period of reconstruction, only shares held by people working in the company would be voting. This would prevent the A.E.I. situation from recurring. Non-voting shareholders would have to be patient, but the dynamic impulse given to recovery should make waiting worthwhile. Voting shares would of course become non-voting on retirement or death. But as the employees would have a great incentive to get dividends up, the non-voting shareholders would automatically benefit.

Function and ownership might also be separable when a business passes from the entrepreneurial to the second phase. It might be an idea if entrepreneurial company structures were to provide for this formally. It may often be good for the overall economy.

Let me give some examples:-

EXAMPLE A; Tim Waterstone created a large nation-wide bookshop chain out of nothing almost overnight. He then sold out. I do wonder if he did this quicker than he need have done from his own point of view. But from the standpoint of the economy it may have been a good thing. Note that he did try to *buy the company back* much later on.

EXAMPLE B; Equally striking is the case of the fibreglass-plastic entrepreneur Ernest Bader, as already mentioned. (page 137)

EXAMPLE C; Volkswagen was created under Hitler, an embarrassing fact quickly glossed over. It was nationalized. This didn't stop the company from expanding very rapidly. Not only was the design of the car such as to keep going for many years. Volkswagen was unusual in having only one model, for quite a while. This made for very significant economies of scale. For many years it's management functioned as if they were entrepreneurs, but they had no ownership. It was finally privatized.

EXAMPLE D; The Moscow Metro was built in conditions of universal state ownership. I haven't had time to check out which Soviet engineer was in charge. But who ever he was, he was obviously an entrepreneur. I suspect he largely determined where the lines went and where stations would be. Certainly he must have **imagined** all that, as a preliminary to building it. This surely can't have been done by some committee – *simply because it was built so quickly!* A committee would have taken at least another year, probably two. This entrepreneur never *owned* the railway. But he surely exercised the entrepreneurial function, did he not? No other explanation fits the case. Did he ask Stalin what to do?

I think I can imagine Stalin replying, "Don't pester me with details".

8.5 Eliminating Oligopoly

Really we can no longer tolerate oligopoly. It is the principal cause of stagnation, and as with Soviet Russia, stagnation threatens us all with collapse, if something is not done about it in time. I cannot stress this too much. This has to be the most important task facing contemporary government economic policy.

Voters need to understand that. I do hope that the engaged people who read and understand this book will do all they can to spread this particular piece of "economic knowledge" as widely as possible.

It isn't that we need more competition as some sort of ideal. *Over –large companies are inefficient.* They are difficult to manage. They are highly prone to internal factionalism and excessive office politics. Not only is the management team's attention diverted from the proper work, but in most over-large companies, the management team has long since ceased to work as one. If we have two or three teams in conflict, the best thing would be to have two or three separate companies

As I write, there are some 200 very large companies in the planet. Most of them are American. But America is stagnating. Large parts of the rest of the world are booming. So help is on the way. If Europe could break out of its bureaucratic lethargy, we could look forward to a couple of hundred companies in the E.U., each as large as the top 200 across the Atlantic. But it is important to understand that if we are to improve the planetary level of competition, these must be truly independent European companies, and not American subsidiaries – who *won't* compete with their parents. European policy makers should reflect on this. Can we, for example, nudge existing large American subsidiaries in Europe towards separation from their parents? Maybe ways can be found. One difficulty for large companies in Europe is the multiplicity of languages. Each large company needs to have just one language within the company perimeters. This is not just "communication" – it is also *ideas.*

Different languages embody different philosophical systems, different cultures – which may present problems of compatibility.

In India and in China, there are obviously going to be large companies as large as the top 200 in the U.S. It is only a matter of time. Russia is somewhat smaller but might make a 100 top size companies during this century. More might come in the Moslem world, in Africa and in Latin America.

The important point to grasp is that the world economy does need all these newly emerging maximum size companies to be separately owned, independent and (I suspect) each confined to one continent. It is planet sized multinationals that block the way back to real competition. Something will have to be done about the existing ones, and it is vital that we don't allow new ones to become established. Too many planet-sized oligopolies could cause planet-sized stagnation.

There is a way of blocking further planet sized multinationals. This is to make it difficult for large companies to be owned other than by real persons living in the continent in which the company operates. This will be difficult to bring about – but I must stress how important is to achieve an oligopoly-free planet. We are in reach of a world-wide age of plenty. *Only oligopoly is preventing us from getting there in the next 50 or 60 years.* The key thing to grasp is that the existing oligopoly will cease to be an oligopoly if similar sized but *separate* groups emerge outside the U.S!

We can at least start by reducing the number of takeover bids. This is desirable because we need the new maximum sized companies to get to that size by **growth** and not by **merger.** This is *possible*. Example; Air Products got started in World War II and got to its present size, largely I think, by growth.

All we have to do to reduce the number of takeover bids is a company law that requires that shares in publicly quoted companies can only be held by "real persons" – that is to say, private individuals, and never any more by other corporations. (A separate class of non-voting shares would need to be established for insurance companies to acquire.)

The basic law that henceforth only real persons could buy plc shares could be passed overnight. Please, governments, do it **now.** Conglomerates need to be broken up. They serve no economic purpose at all. (They do *not* achieve economies of scale.) A simple rule will stop that. Wholly owned subsidiaries must trade in the parent companies name. And names bought to retain goodwill must be made available to management buyouts of the subsidiary, so that it becomes an independent company once again. Once it is independent, the law on only real person shareholders will enable it to stay independent. (If no management buyout can be arranged, the goodwill name must be totally abandoned, including as a trademark – ruthless. Yes, but necessary.

CASE STUDY; When I was at Fords, a director asked why the then British Motor Corporation has so very many subsidiaries, when Ford of Britain had only two, Ford of Ireland and Lincoln Cars, a retail company selling American Ford models in London.

Central Finance staff were *unable* to find any reason, for retaining subsidiaries at all! Long lists of subsidiary companies seemed to be a sort of corporate status symbol, without value for either management or financial purposes.

It would seem from the above case study that there is no real reason to retain the wholly owned subsidiary company as a corporate institution at all. It could simply be abolished.

Parliament could enact all these reforms overnight. They are really extremely obvious. What are the legislators waiting for? Can they not see the *advantages* of the changes competition would tend to increase

- anyone promoting a takeover bid would have to use *his own money* and not manipulate funds really belonging to shareholders
- companies who needed extra capital would have to pay high dividends to attract real person private individuals *with money.* Behind the scenes manipulation would diminish, and large companies would be much less able to afford "bonuses" to greedy top executives.
- Shareholders of companies with poor profitability would both have the time and find it better to turn their companies around eg by recruiting high powered whizz-kids – who would not be threatened as John Barber was by "short-termist" share sell-outs. Corporate shareholders would no longer exist. *"Real person"* shareholders would have all the power and the same interest in getting back to profitability.
-

Wouldn't all that be good for the economy? A further refinement might be to require *equal* sharing of all *inherited* shares between *all* heirs, "gavelkind" as it used to be termed in Kent. This could often enough clear the way for dividing of over-large companies into separate corporate units.

Large companies often hang on to patents without using them. *Reform of patent law,* perhaps simply by shortening the life of patents, would *increase competition.* The same argument might be applied to trade marks. And the Bill Gates/Apple oligopoly could be torpedoed simply by excluding computer programs from copyright!

Oligopolies are great users of television advertizing. Television advertizing *over-influences* consumers, because it is inconvenient to switch sets off while adverts are on. Ads have an excessively *captive* audience. In the early days of television a simple device was invented in America called the "blab-off"; it automatically switched the TV off while adverts were on and switched TV on when the adverts were over, but left viewers free to watch the adverts if they so wished. This device seems to have been suppressed by oligopoly. TV should be regulated to enable use of blab-off again, which would help reduce oligopolies influence.

Other useful regulations of television advertizing would be –

- drastic limitation of the amount of time devoted to adverts per hour
- an absolute ban on advert intervals during long films
- adverts always to state price clearly , and to state the upper end of any range as well as the lower
- adverts could be banned from using sound.

These reforms would move the television ad market a little bit nearer to the desiderata of "perfect competition". A reform which would reduce pressure on consumers, and restrict mendaciousness, would be to prohibit the TV ad from *making claims.* The advertisement could still invite viewers to visit the advertisers web site to study any claims. These restrictions would help monetary policy. They would tend to increase the propensity to save, somewhat – a useful curb on inflationary pressure.

For small private companies, we should make it *much easier* to start up:-

1) The state should not charge anything for private company registration

2) The state should provide, free of charge, a "minimum" company registration form. (Companies could "add terms" to the standard company form if they wished.)

3) To maintain registration over the years, no fee should be charged and the only document to be required annually from small private companies should be a *clearance* note from the tax authorities to state that tax returns have been filed, each year.

4) Private unquoted companies should not be required to file accounts except with the taxman. (Tax returns are strictly confidential An exception might be made if government subsidies were being sought.) Publicly quoted companies would still have to file accounts, of course.

All that would increase competition at the bottom end of the market.

Appendix; The Quincunx by John Nye

A **quincunx** is a geometric pattern consisting of five points arranged in a cross, four of them forming a square or rectangle and a fifth at its centre. It forms the arrangement of five units in the pattern corresponding to the five-spot on six-sided dice, playing cards, or dominoes.

One of many applications of this concept is the planting of apple orchards, where the fifth tree might be a "Beauty of Bath" to act as a pollinator for the main crop of "Bramleys".

Hence this book has used the central point, or "pollinator" as the entrepreneur, with capital, value, money and policy as the "fruit"

Postscript by John Nye

This version of the book is a first draft and is made available since David and John are both well into their eighties. Between them, this project is seen as "before its too late"! If you have read this far, you will realize it is unfinished! It needed a chapter on the Quincunx concept. But then, when is a book ever "finished"? After it has been read, thoughts may circulate in the reader's minds and stimulate action. The universe changes and evolution proceeds.

I must take responsibility for this book, both its existence, and the fact that it needs a final chapter. Since David began his publishing business in Calais in the 1970s, we have corresponded desultorily. His observations on current affairs always impressed me with insight. In 2012 I persuaded him to "write a book" and this is the result. He is currently devoting his energies to a Bernard Shaw theatre project in Ireland and is happy for this book to go ahead especially for sixth form students. I believe it well worth the study by students, policy makers and practitioners of economics everywhere.

David has no internet connection, and prefers to correspond by mail.

If you wish therefore to commend, comment, question, argue or hopefully not insult him, write to him at

47 Rue du Pont Lottin

62100 Calais France

The French post office offers a service for the next day delivery of printed emails for 99 centimes:-

go to www.laposte.fr/lettreenligne and include the above postal address.

www.ingramcontent.com/pod-product-compliance
Lightning Source LLC
Chambersburg PA
CBHW060855170526
45158CB00001B/368